WRITING HANDBOOKS

Writing COMEDY

FOURTH EDITION

JOHN BYRNE

BLOOMSBURY

Published by Bloomsbury Publishing Plc 2012

1 3 5 7 9 10 8 6 4 2

Bloomsbury Publishing Plc
50 Bedford Square
London WC1B 3DP
www.bloomsbury.com

Copyright © 2012, 2005, 2002, 1999 John Byrne

John Byrne has asserted his rights under the Copyright, Designs and
Patents Act 1988 to be identified as the author of this work.

Fourth edition 2012
Third edition 2005
Second edition 2002
First edition published 1999

ISBN: 978 1 408 14645 3

A CIP catalogue record for this book is available from the British Library

Available in the USA from Bloomsbury Academic & Professional,
175 Fifth Avenue/3rd Floor, New York, NY10010.
www.BloomsburyAcademicUSA.com

Typeset by Margaret Brain
Printed and bound in Great Britain by MPG Books Group Ltd,

Contents

Introduction

Go on then, make us laugh.

The challenge for aspiring comedy writers is as simple or as difficult as that.

While I would never suggest that comedy writing is easy, neither is it the 'hardest job in the world' as some people in the business would have you believe. (I'd imagine people who work on the front line in hospitals, inner city schools or war zones would also beg to differ). In my twenty or more years in the business I have certainly come across some of the classic 'tortured comedy geniuses' but I would have to say that not all the tortured geniuses I know are successful – and not all the successful comedy writers I know are particularly tortured. What the successful ones have managed to do, and what I hope this book will help you to do, too, is combine a little comedy talent with a lot of determination and hard work and put together a career which plays to their strengths while relying on a few tricks of the trade to get over some of the challenges.

You'll note that I promised this book would 'help' you as opposed to 'do it for you', so, as you read through the pages that follow, you'll find each chapter ends with some practical exercises designed to make our journey together a truly collaborative and useful one for you.

Speaking of collaboration, I'd like to take this opportunity to acknowledge the support and expert advice of my editor, Anna Brewer, and my agent, Clare Hulton. I'm also more than grateful to my beautiful partner Lola, my son Pearse, and to all of my family for putting up with me while I have been juggling this book deadline with various other writing and work commitments. As your own friends and family may be about to find out, living with a writer isn't always a laughing matter.

This new edition of the book incorporates updates, feedback and improvements from the many people from both the writing and performing sides of the business who were kind enough to make suggestions about what worked best for them in previous editions and what needed to be added to reflect recent developments in the comedy and media worlds. I have also tried to use examples of comics and comedy shows from both sides of the Atlantic which, if you are not already familiar with them, will be relatively easy to research via the internet. I'd be absolutely delighted if, by the time we do the next edition, your own successful career is one of the examples we refer to.

For now, if you have something to write with, and your sense of humour to hand, please turn the page and let's get on with making sure that the only pratfalls in your comedy writing career are intentional ones.

John Byrne
December 2011

1

Can I Learn to Write Comedy from a Book?

Somebody once said that comedy writers and comedians are people who see the funny side of everything – except comedy itself. Certainly wherever comics and writers gather, the question that opens this chapter is often hotly and passionately debated. This question is asked not just in relation to books like this one, but also in relation to the many comedy workshops and courses that have sprung up around the world since the comedy industry became one of the most high-profile and lucrative sectors of the media and entertainment world.

Of course, as with any creative industry, not everyone involved in comedy reaches the dizzy heights of international stardom or multimillion dollar earnings. In fact many of the 'comedians' comedians' or 'comedy writing legends' whom the professionals revere and quote endlessly are not necessarily names the general public or casual fan will recognise at all.

With that in mind, let's begin our discussion with a definition of 'good comedy writing' that is based on a more reliable indicator than recognition or commercial success.

Good comedy writing is whatever makes us laugh.

Yes, good comedy writing can also make us think, make us look at life from a different perspective and occasionally bring a genuine tear to our eyes. There's also a body of medical opinion to suggest that good humour can go further still – improving our physical health, reducing our stress levels, and perhaps even working wonders for our love lives.

As we have already noted, from Richard Pryor to Ricky Gervais, Eddie Murphy to Eddie Izzard and *The Flintstones* to *The Simpsons*, there's certainly no doubt that a talent for writing, performing or even drawing funny material can lead to fame, fortune and a place in the history books.

But all of that comes later, if it comes at all.

For now, whether you are a complete beginner at comedy writing or have been in the business for years and years, the main task before you remains the same as always: to stare at a blank sheet of paper or an empty electronic screen and try to put something on it that makes the audience laugh.

So how do you learn to do this? Well, if you wanted to be a motor mechanic, the best starting point would probably be to study the inner workings of an engine and try to discover what makes it tick. If your aim is to be a doctor you'll probably spend a lot of time studying the human body to see how it works (and even more importantly what goes wrong when it doesn't). That being the case, a good place to start learning to create laughter would be to take a close look at our sense of humour and try to work out what the actual mechanics involved in producing that wonderful and potentially lucrative sound might be. This isn't quite as straightforward as stripping down an engine or dissecting a body. While most engines operate on broadly similar scientific principles and most human beings are put together in roughly the same way, senses of humour tend to behave a bit more subjectively.

What makes me laugh may not make you laugh, and vice versa. And even if we do find something that makes us both laugh, as many comedy writing teams will testify, this still isn't a cast-iron guarantee that it will have the same effect on an audience.

To make things even more complicated, why exactly we are equipped with a sense of humour in the first place, and what specific purpose laughter fulfils in the human make-up are questions for which neither science nor medicine have so far come up with any definitive answers.

There are theories of course – some people believe that as we humans are the only living creatures who have advance knowledge that we are going to die, we have been given a sense of humour as a sort of consolation prize to stop us going insane. Another theory presents laughter as part of our body's response to danger, a release of tension which prevents us being frozen with fear and unable to escape from marauding dinosaurs or whatever their modern equivalent might be.

Comedians themselves have of course had lots to say on the subject, from the philosophical ('You can turn painful situations around through laughter. If you can find humour in anything, even poverty, you can survive it' – Bill Cosby) to the whimsical ('Laughter is the shortest difference between two people' – Victor Borge). My own favourite definition of a laugh is less earnest but given that it comes from Ken Dodd, one of Britain's greatest stand-up comedians for over fifty years, it probably carries a lot more comic authority: 'A laugh is something that comes out of a hole in your face . . . anywhere else and you're in dead trouble.'

Laughter is certainly an *involuntary* reaction – if we hear or see something which strikes us as funny we just can't help laughing. It doesn't matter whether we are in an important meeting, in the middle of a vital exam, at a funeral or anywhere else where bursting into laughter is the last thing we should be doing – in fact the more we know that we *shouldn't* laugh the more uncontrollable our tendency to laugh tends to become. Conversely, like an insomniac desperately trying to fall asleep, the harder we try to make ourselves laugh the more unlikely it is that we will manage so much as a giggle.

Unfortunately the same phenomenon also applies when we are trying to make other people laugh. Although no comedian likes to be booed off stage most will agree that even more demoralising is the forced sound of one or two lonely 'sympathy laughs' that only adds to the embarrassment and emphasises even more starkly that a comedy routine is dying a slow, painful and silent death.

So, as comedy writers how can we avoid being responsible for failed comedy routines, dud sketches and sitcoms which are doomed from the pilot episode? The simple answer is that we can't. Comedy writing, even more than other forms of professional writing, is a never-ending process of hit and miss. What's more, it's a hit-and-miss process where the majority of the 'missing' is likely to happen in front of an audience.

I may think I have written a good routine or script, the comedian or production company which has paid good money for it may think it is a good routine or script, but none of us can know for sure that it works until the audience hears it and laughs at it. And if they don't laugh at it the first time they hear it, there is very little point in trying it again in front of that particular audience.

The consequences of a failed comedy routine aren't quite as terminal as a botched high-wire or knife-throwing act. Nevertheless, the role of a comedy writer can be likened to that of a stunt arranger overseeing the preparation of a difficult or dangerous stunt. Both kinds of activity involve a degree of risk – to life and limb in one case, to the ego (not to mention the writer's chances of getting hired again) in the other. In both acts it is impossible to eliminate the element of danger entirely. In fact it wouldn't be a good idea to do so – if everyone could tightrope-walk there would be no fun in watching somebody else do it. And if we could make ourselves laugh at will, we wouldn't need to pay somebody else to do it for us.

What the stunt arranger does, and what a good comedy writer should do too, is use all of their technical skills and experience to reduce the element of risk for the performer and increase the chances of success as much as possible. At the same time they need to make sure that the mechanics of what they are doing are sufficiently disguised to make the whole show seem as wild, dangerous and unpredictable as can be.

Just like a successful stunt, good comedy material may be over and done with in one big laughter explosion, but it is usually the result of a lot of homework and preparation behind the scenes. So the first step in doing our own homework on how to make people laugh is to take just one person and see what makes that particular person laugh. And the easiest person to start off with is likely to be yourself.

Think back over the last seven days and try to jot down a list of all the things that made you laugh. I don't just mean the comedy you have laughed at, the jokes you have heard or read or the shows you have watched on TV. In fact you may find that most of the things that made you laugh the hardest were not 'manufactured' comedy at all.

You may have gone for a drink with old school friends or work colleagues and laughed yourselves sick over some incident that happened years ago.

Or you may have laughed inwardly at the office when some colleague you don't particularly like suffered a computer crash or spilled coffee all over their desk.

Or perhaps you laughed bitterly to yourself as the new rent bill flopped onto your doormat or pinged into your inbox just when you'd spent the last of your salary paying off the previous one.

Bitter laughs, happy laughs, nasty laughs – each and every laugh counts for research purposes.

Obviously I don't know exactly what made you laugh this week or what kind of laughter it was. But if you look over your list of laughter-making incidents and I take a look at mine, we should be able to identify one or two common elements which seem to encourage laughter in most people at one time or another. These are elements we can make use of in our own comedy writing.

Surprise

I've already mentioned laughter as a natural response to fear and it is not hard to find instances of laughter as a common first reaction to the unexpected. There is, for example, the delighted laughter of the 'victim' of a surprise party or the childish laughter caused by running up behind somebody and shouting 'Boo!' Even when major accidents and disasters occur, uncontrollable laughter is almost as common a symptom of shock as floods of tears.

For the comedy writer surprise is probably the most commonly used 'instant laughter' tool. It may be an unexpected development in a sitcom script: 'You mean that when I overheard you plotting to murder me, you were actually rehearsing a play?' (Of course that particular plot device has now been used so often it usually isn't a surprise any more.)

'One-liners' are often created by using the element of surprise: all we need to do is give a new and unexpected ending to a familiar phrase or well-known saying:

Mary had a little lamb. Her gynaecologist had a heart attack.

If at first you don't succeed, maybe skydiving's not for you.

The usual way to set up a surprise when writing jokes is to keep a vital piece of information to the very end so that it changes the way we understand the story:

My kid was banned from the local sports centre for peeing in the swimming pool. I told them they were being unfair because lots of kids pee in swimming pools.

They said, 'Yes they do – but not from the high diving board.'

Our brain hears a familiar phrase or imagines a familiar picture and then at the last second something unfamiliar is added. Result: surprised laughter. We'll be using the element of surprise a lot to produce comedy in later chapters.

Like all comedy tools, surprise works best when it is not over-used. A common fault of novice comedy writers (and many established ones when fatigue sets in) is to latch onto one particular device and use it repeatedly until the audience can see what's coming a mile off and the jokes lose the very element of surprise that made them work in the first place. A more sensible approach is to stock up your comedy toolbox with a variety of different tricks, so that if one technique doesn't work with a particular audience perhaps the next one will.

Observation and recognition

One of the reasons why it is possible for one human being to write something that will make an entirely different human being laugh is that whether black, white, male, female or any variation in between, we humans are all more alike than we think we are.

Yet, when it comes to our perceived public humiliations or our most intimate personal habits, most of us seem to believe that we are the only ones that have ever done something this stupid or felt this embarrassed in the entire history of the world. When a writer or a comedian reveals that they too have been there and know what it is like to have felt how we feel, the result is the warm laughter of recognition.

When the first wave of so-called 'observational comics' began performing in comedy clubs, audience laughter was a combination of recognition and surprise. The surprise came because here were comedians talking about everyday things (such as the confectionery machines in railway stations which never seem to work but always eat your money, or the fancy taps in washrooms which only ever send water up your sleeve or down your trousers instead of where you want it to go) rather than the more obviously 'made-up' stories about crocodiles walking into bars or cartoonish 'mother-in-law from hell'-type jokes which until then constituted standard joke material.

The recognition factor kicks in because everyone can relate to the feelings triggered when we get money trapped in a vending machine and are torn between drawing attention to ourselves with our increasingly fruitless efforts to retrieve it or the alternative of giving up and trying to pretend that we didn't need the money or the chocolate in the first place. Anyone who has returned from the washroom wetter than they went in knows the dilemma of wondering whether to ignore the stain in the hope that everyone else will too, or to give a long explanation for the damp patch which is only likely to make people wonder if what actually happened was far more embarrassing.

Even if we have never experienced those specific scenarios ourselves, it is almost certain that some similar public humiliation has occurred at some point in our lives. Although most of us know that humiliating feeling, not all of us can express it in words, and when a comedy writer can capture it, we respond with delight – firstly, because somebody else knows how we feel, and secondly, because it turns out that we are not the only ones in the world who feel the same way.

Actually observational comedy has never been particularly new. Even the more 'old-fashioned' jokes it supposedly replaced were often themselves disguised commentaries based on observing human nature:

A crocodile walks into a city bar and orders a whisky.

'That will be ten pounds,' says the barman. 'You know, we don't often get talking crocodiles in here . . .'

'At ten pounds for a shot of whisky I'm not surprised.'

This old joke is less of an observation on the drinking habits of crocodiles (or whichever creature the comic chooses to tell the story about) and more a comment on the overpricing still common in city bars today.

Now that audiences are far more attuned to observational comedy, the warning given earlier about not overusing one particular comedy element applies to this type of material in spades.

'Have you ever noticed that airline staff are rude/taxi drivers love to talk/men always leave the seat up after using the toilet, etc., etc.?'

The trouble is that by now everyone *has* noticed, either for themselves or because comedians are always pointing these things out. Even the phrase 'have you ever noticed' has itself become as much a comedy cliché as jokes about mothers-in-law used to be.

This is not to suggest that there isn't scope for new fresh observational comedy. The UK's Michael McIntyre and US comedy legend Jerry Seinfeld are two examples of comics who continue to generate observational material that feels fresh and personal and yet resonates with a very broad-based audience. A talent for picking up on the more quirky and ridiculous aspects of life is always going to be a big asset to any writer, but as well as simply identifying and observing subjects for humour, which is something everyone can do given enough time, you then have to come up with something *funny* to say about them.

A good, and sadly not unique, example of how not to do it is a comedian who shall remain nameless but whose recent showcase appearance went something along these lines: 'Dogs . . . now, dogs are funny, aren't they? Yes, funny things, dogs. And traffic wardens – what kind of person becomes a traffic warden, eh? And what about those reality shows? There are some funny people on those shows . . .' And so on over a whole range of general 'observations' without one single line or opinion that could in any way be described as original let alone comic.

There are, of course, some comedians who could pull off this kind of material based on sheer force of personality, or perhaps present it 'in character' as a parody of bad observational comedy. Sadly this particular performer fell into neither category – and the one observation that everybody at the showcase was able to make was that nobody was rushing to book him afterwards.

Striking the right balance between being so general that there is nothing new about your observations and so specific that your experiences don't connect with anyone else is something you will only get a feel for by trying out material in front of an audience, and few of us get it right first time. By the time you are reading this, our showcase friend may well have given up comedy performing altogether – but my hope is that he has learned from the experience, refined his material, and is now back on the circuit as one of the hottest new acts around.

If there were any professional comedy writers in the showcase audience they would certainly have been able to help with that refining process, and the better the comedy writer, the less obvious the tweaks to the original routine would have been.

Being able to tailor other people's observations and experiences to a wider audience or a specific medium is one of the most useful skills a comedy writer has to offer the industry. Often the changes needed are very small indeed. Certainly some cultural and personal details might not be immediately understood by somebody from a different background – but it's part of the comedy writer's job to adapt the joke into a form that as many people as possible will understand.

Often just one extra line of explanation or one visual gesture is all that is needed and, once that is added, the basis of a good joke or story is usually more universal than we might assume. Some years ago I was involved in putting together *The Junction Box* – the first comedy series for BBC World Service Radio. The challenge was to make one show which would appeal to the many vastly different cultures and countries served by the BBC's international arm. Our solution was simply to bring together humorists from a wide variety of cultures and backgrounds and give them a shared topic to discuss. Instead of going for overtly comedic subjects we went for very ordinary ones. Much of the laughter that resulted came from realising that not only do overprotective mothers or bad drivers exist in almost every part of the world, they all seem to behave in exactly the same way no matter what their country and culture or origin.

Whatever your own background and culture, and regardless of whether you are starting your own writing career at sixteen or sixty, you already have a lifetime's worth of personal observation and experience to use as raw material for your comedy and, as you start to draw on it for your work, you may be surprised at how some of the stuff you thought was most personal to you turns out to be the material that strikes a chord with a much wider audience than you expected.

Power

Power and powerlessness as well as superiority and inferiority are key elements that surface in comedy all over the world and in many guises. In some ways humour based on power is very like the humour of recognition in that it aims to create a connection between the audience and the performer. But whereas humour based on shared experience encourages us to join together and laugh at ourselves, power-based humour is often more to do with us laughing at other people. We may still bond with the performer, but the bonding tends to be into a group called 'Us' which excludes the butt of our joke: people or groups in that other category known as 'Them'.

'They' may be people who we feel are either less powerful than our group or more powerful than our group. But whichever side of the power divide our group falls into, it is usually exaggerating that perceived divide that creates the humour.

An audience laughing at the antics of a circus clown slipping on a banana skin or at Mr Bean hiding various items of unwanted food under the crockery at a dining table can feel a sense of superiority knowing that in the same situation they would never do anything so ridiculous (although most of us also know deep down that we are very capable of doing equally illogical and stupid things given half the chance).

While comic characters are specifically created for us to laugh at, an equally common and much less 'politically correct' use of power-based humour is the derogatory joke told about minority groups. This kind of comedy is usually based on, and therefore perpetuates, the worst and hoariest cultural stereotypes. In these jokes, all Irish people are stupid, drunk and violent, all Scottish people are mean, all French people are rude and patronising, all Americans are brash, and so on. There are very few countries which don't have stereotypes thrown at them from one direction or another.

It is interesting that the same jokes often turn up word for word all over the world, the only differences being a new target for the insult depending on who is telling the joke.

Have you heard about the Irishman who tried to blow up an ocean liner?

He burned his lips on the funnel.

What's the definition of Eternity?

Sitting in an Edinburgh pub waiting for someone to buy the first round.

In Ireland, where I come from, we often complain about being the traditional butt of British humour . . . and then tell exactly the same type of joke about people who come from County Kerry in the southern part of the country. These 'Kerryman' jokes are just as likely to turn up in Canada, except that there they will be told about 'Newfies' (people from Newfoundland). Nor do Scottish people have the monopoly on being accused of tightfistedness. In America Jewish people have been similarly caricatured, while in Nigeria people from Ijebu district have found themselves on the receiving end of similar put-down humour (often via jokes identical to the ones told about Scottish and Jewish people).

Comics, writers and cultural commentators spend a lot of time discussing what is or isn't acceptable in terms of this type of humour. For instance, is a joke based on ethnic stereotypes still offensive if it's told by somebody who is a member of the same ethnic group? If it isn't OK for white people to make jokes about ethnic minorities, is it OK for comedians from ethnic groups to make jokes about white people?

These issues are outside the scope of a humble comedy writing guide. Where you draw your own 'power lines' is very much up to you, but there is one group everyone seems allowed to have a pop at. From politicians to celebrities, humour which pokes fun at public figures has been popular since the beginning of history. Like the medieval jesters who were the only ones allowed to insult the rich and powerful and get away with it, writers can often express views about the powerful and influential using comedy which would be very hard to get away with if conveyed in any other form.

Embarrassment

We have already touched on the laughter which is generated when we suddenly realise that some revolting personal habit we thought was ours alone is not only being talked about openly on stage or on screen, but is also something other people get up to. (Even more fun, of course, is the expression which crosses a new comic's face when they mention some appalling quirk they *think* other people are going to recognise and relate to and realise too late that this particular one is unique to them.)

It's fairly obvious that laughter is one of our natural responses to embarrassing situations and social taboos – otherwise farting, swearing and double entendres wouldn't be such frequently used tools in the comedy repertoire.

However, just like comedy itself, embarrassment can be a very subjective thing. What one person or social group considers to be a swear word may be just part of general conversation to another. One version of 'polite society' may hold to the belief that farting or belching in public is one of the most disgusting things you can do; other cultures may not understand what all the fuss is about. The same people who would never think of 'breaking wind' in public might not give a second thought to showing the soles of their feet or shaking hands with the left hand or doing whatever other 'innocent' activity another culture may feel shows an appalling lack of good manners.

Many songs, movies and comedy routines which would have been considered 'for adults only' or banned outright in previous years can now be watched and listened to freely by all the family. Sometimes, without actually going back in time to research the morals of the original era, it can be very hard to work out what was so offensive about them in the first place.

However, the fact that much older material which once derived its humour from being 'daring' but which is now extremely tame can still be enjoyed for its comedy value is evidence that it is not usually embarrassing words or actions in themselves that generate the laughter. What really creates a sense of tension and a sense of 'naughtiness' is the combined skills of the writer and performer in setting up and reacting to the situations depicted.

Much comedy in previous decades worked on the basis of the comedian building up tension by appearing to be just about to say the unsayable and then turning that tension into laughter by taking an unexpected turn at the very last minute. ('She's got a lovely pair of . . . eyes!' is just one example of this kind of comedy.)

The British *Carry On* series of movies, America's many *Police Academy* outings and TV shows such as *Are You Being Served?* and *The Benny Hill Show*, which have been hugely popular on both sides of the Atlantic, all use this device over and over again. Somebody once described the *Carry On* style of humour as being based on the assumption that the world would come crashing down around our ears if someone actually uttered the word 'knickers'. Now that 'knickers' is an everyday term and virtually nothing is unsayable or unshowable, it would be reasonable to assume that this type of humour would no longer be effective. However, the better episodes of all the above series and movies can still raise a chuckle, simply because the writing sets up the sense of tension so well, and the actors convey the appropriate sense of outrage and horror at the 'shocking' things that happen in a suitably comedic way.

The Farrelly brothers are one team who – at least in mainstream cinema – were at the forefront of pushing the envelope in terms of what could be shown rather than suggested on screen. In movies like *There's Something about Mary* scenes which would probably have only been suggested in previous eras (such as a very nasty zipper-related injury to the hero's manhood) were shown on camera. However, the best of the Farrellys' work backs up the grossness with strong and often surprisingly warm stories and characterisations, an ethos which has also contributed to the success of movies like Todd Phillips's *The Hangover* and Judd Apatow's *Knocked Up* which followed in their wake. (For examples of 'gross-out' movies which don't underpin the grossness with good writing, the best place to look is the 'straight to DVD' section of your local media outlet because that is where the majority tend to end up.)

The *South Park* series is an example of a long-running TV series presented in the same 'nothing is sacred' vein, but the fact that it has survived umpteen series is an indication that, despite the simplicity of the graphics, there is something going on underneath which is at least a little more thought out than the many *South Park* imitators which have come, gone and been forgotten.

Speaking of imitators, one comedy success which sparked a whole army of zombie clones was *Shaun of the Dead*, the Edgar Wright movie which pitted Simon Pegg and Nick Frost in their personas from the cult TV series *Spaced* against an army of reanimated corpses. While the emphasis was very much on comedy, it did not shy away from on-camera gore. However, its ability to scare and amuse in equal measure also stemmed from the maker's understanding that, in general, what is most scary is what happens in the viewers' imaginations rather than what the special effects department can come up with.

In comedy there's a lot to be said for letting the audience do the work. For years it was a common convention for American radio comedians to refer to 'the joke about the farmer's daughter and the travelling salesman', which was allegedly the world's rudest joke. There are of course many jokes about farmers' daughters and travelling salesmen, some of which you may have heard or read before, but I can assure you that whatever joke you may be thinking of as you read this, the joke I am referring to above isn't that one – for the simple reason that this particular joke about the farmer's daughter and the travelling salesman doesn't actually exist.

Like the fearful 'knickers' word in the *Carry On* movies, the point of the joke was that it was the worst possible joke to tell at any given time. When a potential son-in-law was asked to tell his beloved's nephew a bedtime story and picked 'the one about the farmer's daughter and the travelling salesman', we immediately knew that wedding bells were probably no longer on the horizon. When the aforementioned nephew handed in the story of the farmer's daughter and the travelling salesman for the school essay competition we could tell a trip to the principal's office was on the cards. The only thing we can never find out is what actually happens in the story of the farmer's daughter and the travelling salesman as no scriptwriter could come up with something which lives up to the unspeakable rudeness the listener has already created in their own imagination.

Another form of humour based on embarrassment is the 'sick' joke which tends to spread like wildfire by word of mouth, social media or text message, in what can seem like seconds after some awful event hits the headlines. Whether it's a plane crash, an earthquake or a terrorist attack, the sick jokes usually start flying before the debris has even settled. Often it is the same 'all-purpose' sick jokes which are recycled for every new tragedy. 'How do we know (name of bomb victim) had dandruff? Because they found his head and shoulders in the rubble' is a typical example which I first heard many years ago and have heard several times since, and which will no doubt be doing the global rounds by tweet and email once again whenever another fatal bomb goes off in the future.

If we're honest, most of us have two responses to this kind of humour – 'that's sick' being the first one. The second is to laugh guiltily at the cleverness and audacity of the gag, usually before we look for someone else we can repeat the joke to.

How well shock humour works in your own writing depends very much on the situation, the audience and the style of the individual performer you are working with. There are certainly many comics and writers who make shock humour their stock in trade. For the working comedy writer shock, like the element of surprise, is best viewed as just one among several techniques that can be brought into play. If it becomes too predictable, the power to shock drains away and the law of diminishing returns can kick in very quickly.

In discussing this topic, it's worth noting that swearing and shocking are two different things. I've heard very adult routines which might have no swearing in them but you certainly wouldn't want to repeat in front of your grandmother. (Or maybe you would if your grandmother was like Betty White the octogenarian comedy actress from *The Golden Girls* and *Hot in Cleveland*, whose habit of saying outrageous things, despite appearing utterly innocent, has made her a huge hit with audiences of all ages.)

A much more common phenomenon, especially on the beginners' circuit, is the comedian or writer who wouldn't dream of swearing in their everyday life but thinks that shoehorning a swear word into every second or third line on stage is going to magically make weak material funnier or edgier.

Remember also that topics which have 'shock value' for one audience may not have the same effect on others and vice versa. Sex is generally a subject that still has taboo potential at various levels in most situations, although what was 'for adults only' even a few years ago is often on daytime television these days. Religion and politics are two other topics that we were once warned 'never to discuss in polite society'. Times have changed there too. In the Ireland I grew up in, and in many predominantly Catholic parts of America or Europe, jokes about the Catholic church or the Pope were once considered very daring. Following various church scandals and due to the general secularisation of society, this is much less the case than it used to be.

In Britain even the most innocent jokes about the royal family were once considered incredibly daring, but this would certainly not be the case now. In fact the general tone of the humour directed at the royals has moved through a full revolution from the deference of the 1950s, through the vicious puppet lampooning in the 1980s TV series *Spitting Image* to, in more recent times, a more affectionate poking of fun at Prince Charles's interest in all things holistic and architectural and Prince Harry's reputation as a 'wild child'.

Whereas jokes about politics and politicians have always been fair game, it is now not uncommon to see world leaders such as British Prime Minister Tony Blair actually take part in shows like *The Simpsons* while still in office, or to have US President Obama appear on the satirical *The Daily Show*. Making people laugh these days is obviously recognised not only as good business but also as good politics.

If there are subjects which are no longer as offensive as they used to be, there are also subjects which over the years have become more offensive. As we discussed earlier, many of the jokes freely told about women, ethnic minorities and disabled people in previous decades, often on prime time television and usually by white male comedians, would be considered extremely offensive today.

That phenomenon in itself has allowed writers like Ricky Gervais and Stephen Merchant to use the 'ironic' approach to create genuine shock for audiences who may have considered themselves unshockable – a good example being David Brent's cringeworthy treatment of disabled and ethnic minority co-workers in the UK version of *The Office*.

Of course, we can justify our laughter by claiming that it is Brent's ignorance we are laughing at rather than the disability or ethnicity, but it can also be argued that the character's lack of understanding of what is 'politically correct' and what isn't is poking fun at the whole idea of 'political correctness' itself.

For the comedy writer, demarcations such as 'clean' or 'dirty' comedy are a bit like trying to define 'men's' or 'women's' comedy – very subjective and not ultimately very useful. There is really only 'comedy that works' and 'comedy that doesn't' and the moral decisions you make about how offensive or not you choose to be in your own writing are entirely up to you. But as with any other aspect of the business, you have a better range of options if you make a conscious effort to expand your horizons.

If you can genuinely come up with funny material without constant swearing and references to bodily functions it can only expand the range of markets in which you can work. If you can't – and admittedly some types of character and comedy do lose their edge when 'cleaned up' – at least you know what areas you need to stick to. But if you don't even try to diversify, remember that the dirtiest four-letter word of all in terms of developing a writing career is 'lazy'.

Absurdity

By now you may have worked out that I am quite keen on humour that is based on truth and draws on real human experience and emotion.

So why do I giggle every time I think of the man named Warren who had five rabbits up his bottom? Or the one about two peanuts walking down the street, one of which was assaulted.

Comedy, as you'd expect, is full of contradictions, and although truth in comedy is effective, the stupid idea, crazy visual image

20

or really terrible pun delivered when we least expect it are just as likely to generate laughter even when the audience is sober.

One of the roles of the comedian is to deflate human pomposity, but as we comics and writers are human ourselves, we are just as prone to getting all deep and meaningful about our work as the next person. It is always good therefore to give ourselves the freedom to introduce the occasional absurd or stupid gag into the mix.

When we start looking at joke writing in Chapter Three there will be plenty of opportunities to let your imagination run wild on daft ideas as well as clever ones. It's interesting to note how many times comedy writers come up with really wild and absurd gags during brainstorming sessions and then throw them out on the basis that 'the joke is too silly – it will never work'. I know – I have done it myself and then heard another comic or writer get a huge laugh with a similar gag. And guess who feels silly then?

Character

Good characterisation is one of the most important factors to bear in mind when writing comedy and also the one that is most often forgotten, with dire consequences not just for first attempts at comedy writing, but for quite a few big-budget TV sitcoms too. When a series is 'not as good as it used to be' it is often because the writers have forgotten who the characters they originally created used to be, and what made them connect with viewers in the first place.

Character is often the element which turns something that is not intrinsically funny into something that raises a laugh, as well as the ingredient that allows us to use the same comedy tools like surprise, observation, shock and the others over and over again and still have them come out differently every time.

For example, whenever I get together with my old school friends one of the topics that is guaranteed to keep us laughing is remembering a particular school nature walk many years ago, when we all took a wrong turn and ended up in a swamp.

Obviously I don't expect you to fall about laughing at what was a minor and relatively common school trip incident, but I'm sure you can understand how it still seems funny to those of us who were actually there.

No, the bit that will make you laugh too is knowing that *Mr Kelleher* was the teacher in charge of the trip!

OK, so maybe it *won't* make you laugh. But that's because you and I weren't at the same school, so you won't have met Mr Kelleher. If you had sat through his many long-winded stories about how good he was on the sports field, with maps, and at exploring, you'd probably have enjoyed his comeuppance as much as we did – leading us boldly onward, deeper and deeper into the murky water, still insisting he knew what he was doing. That's why even my old schoolmates who weren't actually on that particular trip can still get a good laugh out of it, because they did know Kelleher well and could therefore picture exactly how he would have behaved.

Now, if it had been Mr Malone the science teacher leading the trip, we might well have got lost in the very same fashion but there is no way he would have led us into a swamp. Knowing how genuinely scary Malone was he would have sent *me* into the swamp first to check how deep it was.

My point is that while an incident or story may be mildly amusing in itself, it's knowing the characters involved which really makes the difference to how funny it seems to you.

With that in mind, as writers it is important for us to be able to create characters that the audience can get to know very quickly. Once we have established the character we can then tailor the stories and other material we write for them accordingly. Long-running sitcoms and long-established stand-up characters can often reach the point where the first line that comes out of their mouth, whether funny or not, gets a huge anticipatory laugh for reasons only understandable to someone who already knows their character.

As we have already noted, long-standing sitcoms also start to lose popularity when well-loved characters start to act and speak in ways that their loyal audience finds unfamiliar or just plain unbelievable. Sometimes you will know exactly what kind of jokes work best for a particular character as soon as you have created them. Sometimes this happens as both the writer and the performer playing the character develop it together.

When you do develop a strong character or group of characters, they will almost write your sketches and scripts for you.

Take any common situation from history or literature: let's say Noah building the ark. Now replace the Noah character with Rowan Atkinson's Mr Bean. How would this change the story? Well, maybe Mr Bean would come up with all kinds of insane and ingenious ways to use the animals as part of the building process, perhaps using woodpeckers to hammer in the nails, a hedgehog in place of sandpaper, and an elephant's trunk to hoover up the sawdust. Having built the ark and got the animals on board he would probably then manage to lock himself outside.

Now let's try a different character in the Noah role, perhaps one based on a real-life person, like Malone, that scary science teacher of mine. You can bet he wouldn't end up building the ark himself – he would talk some other unsuspecting soul into doing it for him.

Once you've established the character you can take the sketch in a number of different directions. You could work on a twist ending where it's Noah/Malone who gets what is coming to him. Or you could go in the opposite direction and play up the gullibility of his victim to the 'nth' degree – still working away merrily on the ark as the water rises up to his armpits.

If you combined these two scenarios, so that the victim Malone picked on to build the ark for him was Mr Bean, the audience would be laughing even before the building started because, knowing Bean's character, they would be pretty sure the building work wouldn't go according to plan.

Many characters on shows like *Little Britain* or *Saturday Night Live* work by identifying one character trait and exaggerating and repeating it in any situation the character finds himself in.

In *Little Britain*, the audience knows that David Walliams's Lou character isn't aware that Matt Lucas's Andy doesn't actually need the wheelchair he so selflessly wheels him around in. Whether they are at the airport or the swimming pool or anywhere else, the part of the sketch we all look forward to is the point where Andy leaves the wheelchair and, unbeknown to Lou, performs some highly mobile activity only to return to the chair just in time to avoid being spotted. It is the exact opposite of 'surprise' humour – we know what is going to happen in advance, and the anticipation is in wondering how and when it is going to happen.

Taking the plunge

Surprise. Embarrassment. Silly ideas. This is by no means a definitive list of the keys to good comedy writing. These are just some of the things that make me laugh and some of the elements I try to build into my own writing. Hopefully some of the things here will also appeal to you.

In your own writing you may be heavily into clever word play and witty challenging perspectives on intellectual ideas – maybe too many silly jokes irritate rather than amuse you. Or perhaps you like writing dialogue and word-based jokes but it is actually visual humour, slapstick and mime which float your personal boat. Maybe you are inspired by the timeless wit and charm of the classic comedians such as Bob Hope, Jack Benny, Tommy Cooper or Tony Hancock. Alternatively you may want to take your place on the cutting edge and be the next Bill Hicks or Chris Rock.

Then again, you may just enjoy jokes about bottoms.

Good comedy writing is whatever makes us laugh, and if something makes *you* laugh that's a very good starting point for your individual writing as it will probably make other people laugh too. Even if it doesn't, your work is guaranteed to amuse at least one person and, in the hit-and-miss world of comedy writing, that's about as good a guarantee as you are likely to get.

Which brings us back to the question in the title of our chapter. Can you learn good comedy writing from a book? Or, even more specifically, can you learn good comedy writing from this book? The answer is yes. And no.

Yes, because as we work through this book together I am going to show you many of the practical techniques and tricks which have helped me make a living from my own comedy writing. It's also yes because, in my role as careers advisor for *The Stage* newspaper, I have had the privilege of working with, and speaking to, many successful comedy performers and writers and many of their helpful ideas and suggestions have been incorporated here too.

There is one further 'yes' in that, this being the fourth edition of the book, I have been delighted to hear from a number of comedians, writers, comedy tutors and other performers who have taken the techniques in these pages, applied them to their own work, and found that they made a difference.

But the answer is also 'no' because, whether you are reading this in printed form or as an e-book or on a handheld reading device, you can't learn comedy writing or anything else just from *reading* a book.

Your comedy writing career only starts or develops when you take the ideas and suggestions in the book and put them into practice for yourself. Just like the stunt coordinator you can never completely guarantee success, but through a combination of research, experience and hard work you can certainly maximise your chances of achieving it before you actually take the plunge. In order to help you there are some exercises at the end of this and subsequent chapters to help you turn my words and your words into the concrete actions that will start building your comedy writing career.

The next chapter will look at the various directions in which the comedy journey you are starting here might eventually lead. Each market has its pluses and minuses and each one calls for a different combination of talents. But the one vital thing which every spectacular stunt and every branch of comedy writing requires to have any chance of success is the courage to have a go in the first place.

Over to you . . .

As you read through this book, you will not be surprised to learn that your 'ongoing homework' is to study as much comedy as you can, watching out for the humour potential in everyday incidents or overheard snatches of conversation as well as in 'manufactured' comedy on stage, screen or online.

However, to get the maximum benefit from the book, try to stretch your comedy antennae: by all means remind yourself of your own favourite comedians and shows and try to analyse what techniques and approaches they use to achieve laughter, but do your best also to go beyond your own preferences and tastes and get as broad a perspective as you can on what is working and what is selling in today's comedy world.

Check out current comics and shows which are doing well, even if they are not to your own taste, and ask yourself what they are doing that works for them. Could it work for you in a different context? If you are a big fan of live comedy also spend some time looking and listening to comedy on TV, radio and online. However, if your main source of comedy is the broadcast media, try to get out and see more live comedy whether in a theatre or a comedy club.

What's new? What's different? What would you do to tweak or improve the material you are seeing or hearing? Use your notebook to record your thoughts and ideas as they will come in handy when we start our own practical work in a chapter or two from now.

For those who are really serious about writing good comedy, you might want to consider a technique favoured by the young Bob Monkhouse, now regarded as having been one of the UK's greatest stand-up comedians as well as much in demand as a writer for US comedy greats like Bob Hope when they visited Britain.

At the beginning of his writing career young Bob would listen to his favourite comics and shows on the radio and then laboriously transcribe each routine and episode into his own notebooks line by line. The intention wasn't to copy what his heroes were doing but to be able to study their comedy writing in its original form – as words on the page – so that he could learn how each joke and situation was created on paper and discover the techniques he could use in his own material.

A lot has changed since the 1950s. Today, in the case of most sitcoms, movies and theatre shows, it is usually possible to find the original scripts in printed form. But Bob's story serves as an important reminder that, above all, this is a book about comedy *writing*. No matter how well acted or performed, the comedy you are studying started off as a piece of writing and, as a comedy writer yourself, you will get the most benefit from examining how the writing was put together, analysing it and, most important of all, trying it out for yourself.

2

Finding Your Comedy Direction

For comedy writers, career success can be a double-edged sword.

For one thing, you may have to put up with snide comments from friends, acquaintances and even family members along the lines of 'Now, that's what I call an easy job – nothing to do all day but think up jokes and get paid for it.' Such cracks are obviously very hurtful and irritating to the comedy writer as they do not take into account the long hours spent staring at a blank computer screen or sheet of notepaper, trying to kick-start the brain into coming up with something amusing. They are also hurtful and irritating because for most comedy writers the pay-off received for any money earned is that somebody else gets the credit for our sparkling wit. But most of all they are hurtful and irritating because they are basically *true*.

If you are reading this book you obviously like writing comedy, or at least the idea of writing comedy, and as most people in the world have to spend five or six days a week doing something they don't particularly enjoy to make a living, what easier job is there than to have the opportunity to do something you *do* enjoy and get paid for it?

That attractive career goal is certainly a good motivator to keep you going through the long hours and hard work that building a comedy writing career usually entails. It is also the reason why for every comedy writing opportunity available – even the ones which don't have any payment attached – you will usually find you are but one among many comedy writers jockeying for position. With that thought in mind, there's a separate chapter towards the end of this book on how to market yourself as a comedy writer and to help yourself stand out from the crowd.

But right now, even before we discuss the basic techniques of humour writing so you can start on the journey towards that career goal, it might be a good idea to look at the wide range of markets open to the jobbing humorist.

Besides suggesting a few more avenues to pursue when the time comes to start selling your work, thinking about the different types of comedy writing available to you, both from a preference point of view and from the point of view of your own particular talents, should help you identify what techniques and ideas you'll really want to focus on when you work through the practical sections of this book.

Before we look at individual areas of the comedy writers' market, it's important that we take an overview of how a comedy writing career is likely to work in today's market. Like many other media careers comedy writing has evolved somewhat from the more traditional model many of us fondly remember.

In the previous chapter I used the example of a stunt arranger to describe what a comedy writer does from a creative point of view and as an illustration of how the relationship between the writer and the performer or producer works. In terms of today's comedy writer as a business person, probably the best analogy is the professional songwriter and composer. Like the comedy writer, there are two basic kinds of songwriter – the writer who is also a singer and performer in their own right, and the writer who does not perform themself (at least not to paying audiences) but instead earns a living from providing material for other people to perform.

For many years there were two main routes for songwriters to earn a living from the writing side of their work. If you were a non-singer, you wrote your songs and then tried to sell them to singers who could make them successful for you. If you were a singer-songwriter you might perform the songs yourself, and maybe even hope to become a singing star, but you probably wouldn't object too much if a better known singer picked up some of your songs and made them hit records, as long as you got your credit and royalties.

The main conduit for career success (at least in the commercial sense) for the songwriter was the recording industry and the main goal was either getting a record deal, or getting one's songs recorded by a major recording star who already had a deal. As even non-music fans are aware, this model has changed dramatically in recent years. With the advent of the internet and the download market, a recording deal is no longer the only way a singer or songwriter can reach the large audiences necessary to make a profit from their work. There are still no guarantees of success in the music business any more than there are in the comedy business, but the online boom has created a much wider range of options for writers to earn an income from their work. Today, an aspiring songwriter may still promote their songs to established recording acts and labels but they are also likely to have several other strings to their bow at the same time, such as promoting their music online, composing music for advertisements, video games or other commercial music projects, and using any production skills they may have to do remixes of other people's music to order.

Substitute the broadcast industry for the recording industry and the approach needed by a comedy writer to make a living today is a very similar one. Being able to produce high quality work to order is still very important and developing good relationships with performers and producers who can bring your work to a wider audience is also an essential skill. But being versatile enough to work in a number of different markets at the same time, and being able to balance a couple of different 'income streams', preferably including some 'self-generating' work as well as 'work to order', is by far the best model to strive for if you are aiming to build a sustainable career.

To help you start thinking about which combination of areas might be the best ones for you personally to focus on, let's work our way through the main markets open to today's comedy writer, noting as we go along the specific skills needed for each one.

Television

When most people think about successful comedy writing, television is one of the first markets that springs to mind. Television work has the popular image of being both glamorous and highly paid, and while this isn't always the case (certainly not on some of the shows I have worked on!) there's no doubt that many comedy writers have done very well out of the small screen. Some, like the late John Sullivan, who wrote one of Britain's best-loved sitcoms, *Only Fools and Horses*, have not only made a great deal of money from their work but also gained that all-important 'name recognition' which is normally only achieved by the onscreen cast. Another British writing team, Dick Clement and Ian La Frenais, may still be best known in the UK for hit sitcoms such as *Whatever Happened to the Likely Lads?* and *Porridge* but have also gone on to achieve success (albeit often uncredited) as Hollywood 'script doctors' on a wide range of blockbuster movies. In the USA, Conan O'Brien and Garry Shandling are just two examples of comedy writers whose careers have taken them from behind the cameras to TV shows of their own.

For comedy writers and comedians alike, being able to add the phrase 'as seen on TV' to a poster for a live show, or a proposal for a book or theatre script, does absolutely no harm at all from a sales point of view.

While all of the above is good news in terms of what can be achieved by comedy writers via the television medium, there is an obvious practical consideration to take into account. If, as already noted, there are always more people competing for any comedy writing jobs than there are jobs available, nowhere is this bottleneck more pronounced than in the number of writers aiming to break into the TV market.

There have, of course, always been other factors, ranging from backstage politics to the 'who you know' culture, which make it difficult for a newcomer to break into the TV world, but in recent years this has been compounded by new considerations both economic and artistic.

While television comedy, whether in sitcom or stand-up form, may appear to be bigger business than ever, with the top comics appearing in their own shows and also hosting awards ceremonies and selling truckloads of DVDs of their live tours, the truth of the matter is that TV budgets are getting smaller and the TV medium is facing huge competition for advertising from the internet, smartphones, video games and a whole range of rival media.

Whether or not you agree with the thinking behind the decision, it is understandable, then, that given the choice of putting money into new or untried writers and shows or putting the same money into an established comedy brand with an existing fan base, TV executives are much more likely to opt for the latter. There are certainly still big, flashy variety and game shows on TV which have some comedy elements, but the majority of the schedules tend to favour 'reality' and 'unscripted' TV shows which are not only popular with viewers but also much cheaper to make.

All of the above is not intended to put you off if TV is your ultimate writing goal, but it is to make you aware that it can be an uphill struggle.

However, it is also true that every day new people still do make it into TV either through determination, hard work, a lot of talent and maybe a little bit of luck – or through grovelling, backstabbing and sleeping around. The latter route may seem like a viable shortcut, but bear in mind that it is probably just as competitive as the talent route. Even if it does get you one or two gigs it is very unlikely to keep you working in the long term as the kind of employers who can be swayed by this approach are not notorious for their loyalty.

Given that the hard work and talent route is the more sensible option, there are a certainly a few things you can do to increase your chances of not only making it into television but staying there.

The first is to really get your head round television as it is today, not the way it may have been when your favourite shows and writers got their break, whether that was twenty years or six months ago. In TV terms, the goalposts can change in a matter of weeks let alone months.

Start studying the industry press (more about this in Chapter Six) and know who is commissioning now, which shows are going down well and which shows are falling out of favour. Where are the spots for new shows and try-outs? Often they are found on the cable channels at strange hours and lasting five or ten minutes or even less.

Broaden your focus from pure 'comedy' shows to other types of show which have a comedic element. Or go even further – what shows might benefit from a comedic element if it was introduced? From cookery shows to children's shows, DIY shows to discussion programmes, if you are good at tying your comedy to specific topics, as well as generating a consistent supply of good comedy on that topic, it might be possible for you to break into television by a less obvious route.

I'll be looking at the mechanics of producing scripted comedy for TV later in the book but it is worth noting here that one important factor a good TV writer needs to have is a strong visual sense. This might seem blindingly obvious, but television is about pictures and a lot of rejected TV scripts may be funny and well written but are word rather than picture-based, and would be better suited to radio or print. If wordiness is your own tendency and TV writing is your goal, it would be a good idea to get into the habit now of thinking more visually, or if necessary finding somebody to work with who is a more visual thinker.

Radio

If the TV market has had some dramatic changes in the way it works in recent years, this is even more true of radio. Of all the broadcast mediums radio is probably the one which can truly claim to be the comedy writer's best friend, especially in the early career stages. In fact, on both sides of the Atlantic, it could be argued that radio, even more than film or TV, was the medium that created the comedy writing market as we know it in the first place. From the 1920s and 30s radio brought the big comedy stars of Broadway and the West End into homes in remote mining villages and farmlands and truly turned them into 'household' names. By the 1950s in America and the 1960s in Britain, most of those big radio names had migrated to television. While the BBC in Britain and Public Radio in America carried on the radio tradition, the continuing growth of visual media may have suggested that radio was never going to regain its place as an important comedy medium.

However, the unique ability of radio to create visuals in the listener's mind has ensured that its influence on comedy and comedy careers has continued to remain strong. One reason is simple economics: radio programmes are cheaper to make and producers are therefore more willing to take a chance on untried writers.

Shows such as *Little Britain* and *The League of Gentlemen* are examples of TV hits which actually started life on radio. (Bear in mind that when talking about the BBC or commercial radio here, 'untried writers' means 'untried on radio' – in both of the above cases the performers and writers had established themselves on the live circuit before getting the chance to appear on the national airwaves.)

The reason that most TV scripts are confined to a limited number of sets, actors and locations is simply one of cost. If you come up with a TV sketch about a herd of elephants crossing a ravine on Mars it is either going to cost a lot of money to build a set and possibly hire some elephants or it is going to require some highly-paid CGI technicians taking time off work from *Doctor Who* to digitally create the aforementioned ravine and herd of elephants. If you come up with a radio sketch on the same topic it is not going to cost the production company much more than a sketch set in somebody's living room. More to the point, and with the greatest respect to the talented special effects wizards, the combination of sound effects and the picture created in the listener's imagination will usually make those elephants in the ravine far more believable than TV pictures ever could.

If you are good at creating images and ideas through your words, and if your imagination is wild enough to make use of the endless possibilities that a versatile group of actors and a good sound effects library present, radio may be just the medium for you. It is also interesting to note that both *Little Britain* and *The League of Gentlemen* were very heavily make-up based in their TV versions. It would be well worth aspiring radio writers tracking down the BBC recordings of the original radio shows to see how the same pictures were originally created using sound only.

If we think of 'radio' not just in terms of a small box in the living room or in the dashboard of a car, but in terms of podcasts, phone apps and internet streaming, it may even be that not only is radio back in the limelight but it could possibly supersede TV as the best way to build up a loyal comedy audience. In a world where time is increasingly becoming the most valued commodity because it is the thing most of us have the least amount of, radio has one huge advantage over visual media – we can still listen to radio while we are doing other things rather than having to stop what we are doing to focus on a picture.

In terms of breaking into radio, many of the best known and most successful UK writers and comedians served their radio apprenticeship by submitting material to topical comedy shows like the BBC's *Week Ending*, which, in addition to using paid contributors, had a very agreeable system allowing uncommissioned writers to send in their own jokes for consideration. If you were in London the week before broadcast, it was even possible to attend an 'uncommissioned writers meeting' where the producer would read out the list of topics for the upcoming show and invite everyone to 'have a go'.

Sadly, presumably due to legalities, cutbacks and security concerns about uncommissioned writers wandering around Broadcasting House, those happy days have ended (along with the *Week Ending* show itself) and the best approach now is similar to the one a TV writer needs to pursue.

Step one, as always, is to listen to as broad a range of radio as possible and try to identify potential slots that you can pitch your work to. The broader you can make your thinking in terms of types of show and station, the greater your chances of getting your material used. As with TV, there are two basic types of radio show that feature comedy material. Scripted comedy, whether sketch-based or sitcom style, is obviously an important market for the writer, which is why it has a separate chapter later in the book. However, it is often the incidental opportunities on non-comedy shows which offer the best opportunity for the beginning writer to make their mark.

Talk and music shows are well worth exploring in this regard. Many DJs are on the air for two- or three-hour stretches, five or more days a week, and it's hard for any human being to come up with consistently witty material for that length of time. For most commercial radio stations, 'prime time' is either the breakfast show when their listeners are getting up or the drive-time show when they are returning from work, and it is in these slots that they tend to place their 'star' presenters. These are also the shows which tend to have the biggest share of whatever budget the radio station has to throw at content. In pre-internet days the big-name radio hosts often supplemented their own wit and wisdom with contributions from comedy writers – either based in the studio or faxing in topical jokes from home (the really high-tech writers might even have been using early versions of email!). Several enterprising comedy writers even earned a crust by creating daily and weekly collections of topical jokes and comedy material and selling them to DJs around the world on a subscription basis. As with other markets which preceded social media, this avenue for comedy writing has somewhat imploded now that listeners themselves can easily text, tweet and email their own jokes at no cost to the station.

However, it is still possible for a determined writer to draw attention to themselves this way. The average person in the street may come up with something witty once or twice a week but, as a serious comedy writer, if you can come up with material which is consistently funny, arrives regularly and, most important of all, is well tailored to the DJ's individual style, you might still get invited to contribute to the show on a more formal basis.

Because 'free' guests are just as attractive to most radio shows as free content, if you have an interesting personality as well as good material, you might even be able to persuade the DJ to let you have a regular guest slot, either phoning in at a set time, or actually coming into the studio to do your humorous take on the latest news, sport or some other niche area. If this does happen, remember the first rule of being a comedy sidekick – by all means be funny but, if you want to be invited back on the show, make sure you allow the host to be funnier (even if you have to feed them the lines).

As you can imagine, even on prime-time radio shows the payment for your contributions is likely to be minimal but it is all good exposure for establishing your reputation, getting some credits you can add to your CV, and allowing you to hear how your stuff comes across on the air. And it might just lead to bigger things. The late Dermot Morgan, much loved as the title character in the *Father Ted* TV series, was an excellent comedy scribe in his own right and began his writing career by regularly sending material to an Irish morning radio show before heading off for his day job as a schoolteacher. A more recent example would be Karl Pilkington, originally a radio 'sidekick' to Ricky Gervais and Stephen Merchant, who has now become a TV personality in his own right via his show *An Idiot Abroad*.

Stand-up comedy

Although broadcast comedy may have had its ups and downs as a medium over the past few years, it is certainly still a market where the comedy writer has a chance of developing an income as well as a reputation. In terms of producing an income in itself, writing for stand-up comedians has never been a hugely lucrative area (with a few notable exceptions which we will come to shortly). However, in terms of developing a reputation that can help you break into more financially rewarding work, it is still a market worth considering.

As mentioned above, it was the 'collision' of the stand-up tradition with the new mass mediums of radio and television in the early days of broadcasting which led to the development of comedy writing as a viable career in the first place.

One of the reasons that stand-up comedy is often referred to as 'the hardest job in the world' is that it is actually *two* of the hardest jobs in the world – writing funny and acting funny – performed at the same time. For this reason many sensible and successful comics, including those who are good comedy writers themselves, at some point reach the stage where they need other people to contribute material.

In the USA, not only did all the top comedians from Bob Hope to Jack Benny have teams of writers producing much of their material, they openly acknowledged that they used writers, and the status of a top comedian was often reflected by the number of top-class writers they could afford to keep on their staff. Many of those writers graduated to writing for Hollywood movies and for early sitcoms. That tradition has continued to the present day – comedy in American TV is still big business but rather than being employed by an individual comedian, the top comedy writers get paid to be on the teams which collectively produce shows like *The Office*, *The Simpsons* or *The Tonight Show*.

In Britain, few comics had regular writers, even in the 'golden age' of live variety theatres, and instead they tended to buy jokes for their acts from freelance writers as they needed them. However, comics who managed to make the transition to regular shows on TV or radio would often find themselves paired up with staff writers who then went on to become 'their' writers – the partnership of writer Eddie Braben with celebrated double act Morecambe and Wise is one example of a successful writer/ comedy act 'marriage' which began that way.

As in America, the emphasis in television today is more on show formats than individual performers, which means the money in comedy writing tends to be from writing for production companies rather than working for individual comics.

The rise of what was then called 'alternative' comedy in the 1980s introduced a more 'singer/songwriter' style where many of the star performers made much of the fact that they also wrote their own material.

Although there are many talented stand-up comedians who do write their own material, there are others who are equally funny performers but whose writing just tends to confirm the fact that their principal talent is performing. Not everyone in the latter category would actually admit that fact, but if they do get to the point where an agent or manager feels it is holding them back, you can be sure that focusing on their performing and getting somebody else to provide material is something that will eventually be suggested.

Once a comic gets to the stage where they are regularly appearing on television or other media they will almost certainly be needing writing support, even if they are good writers themselves. When radio and TV comedy were young, one of the biggest shocks to the system for comics who made it onto the nation's airwaves was discovering the extent to which broadcasting new material almost instantly rendered it unusable thereafter.

The great comics of yesteryear tended to tour the music halls and supper clubs on both sides of the Atlantic, honing the same thirty or forty minutes of material over and over again. As long as they spaced out their appearances at particular clubs they could return to those venues again and again and do the same act with the same success. (There are many acts on the live comedy circuit even today who are still doing the same material they were doing when they started out fifteen or twenty years ago.)

Everything changes once that material is broadcast. Back in the days of live broadcasting, comics quickly discovered that audiences didn't appreciate paying to hear jokes that they had already heard last week on the air for free. In today's world of on-demand television, YouTube clips and the hundreds of other ways material is recorded and redistributed, keeping material fresh is even more of a challenge.

Today a young comic can start performing for free in pubs, be signed up by one of the comedy promotion agencies within six months, and be given their own TV show within a year or two – often with not much more material than the hour or so they cobbled together for their original act.

At this point there are three choices. They can continue to write their own material but to a lower standard as there is no time to test and develop it; they can push themselves to keep writing high-quality material in the midst of constantly gigging, broadcasting and promoting themselves – and eventually collapse under the strain of doing so; or they can get other people to write for them. That's where you could potentially come in. If you are good at analysing a comic's act and coming up with material that is not only funny but can also fit seamlessly into their existing routines, you'll be a real asset to the comedian and an even bigger one to the producer who has got to stretch their act into a whole series. Develop a reputation for being able to do this with one comic and you could well be one of the first names that springs to mind when the same producer has to perform a similar feat with next year's hot comedy newcomer.

Attractive as that prospect may sound, there is one very important consideration if you are not a performer in your own right and you are considering working closely with stand-ups. The first question you'll need to ask yourself is whether you genuinely want to be a comedy writer or whether you harbour secret ambitions to be a star in your own right. The basic illusion of stand-up is that the comic is making it up as they go along, so the writer (and often even the very fact that the routine has been written in advance) inevitably takes a lower profile in this form of comedy.

You may be perfectly happy to sit in the wings and bask in reflected glory, but if public recognition is important to you, another form of writing (or doing a stand-up comedy course) may suit you better. However, if you are not particularly concerned about fame but keenly interested in fortune, there is an area closely related to stand-up writing that you may wish to consider, as it is less high profile but often pays better. Let's take a look at that one next.

Speech writing

Most people would never attempt stand-up comedy in a million years, and most people will never have to. Unfortunately, for many of those same people, making a speech in public, whether it is a social or business setting, is an ordeal that holds similar terrors but is far less easy to avoid.

In today's world of the 'sound bite' and the 'spin doctor' it could be argued that for business leaders, politicians and sales people alike, the ability to make a good public impression has never been more important. To a certain extent it is the smooth, confident style of the stand-up comic or TV host which has created the standard picture of what a 'good presentation' looks like to the modern audience.

Whether it is the best man's speech at a wedding or an important corporate presentation, most people know that humour is a great way of creating impact and relaxing the atmosphere. Unfortunately, any last-minute dipping into the nearest available joke book can easily result in gags which either fall flat – only making the ordeal even worse for speaker and audience alike – or, at worst, are disastrously inappropriate. A famous example of the latter occurred when UK discount jewellery entrepreneur Gerald Ratner decided to lighten up a speech to important business leaders with a joke about his products being 'crap'. Whether or not the audience was amused, Ratner's customer base certainly wasn't. When the speech was reported in the papers, the subsequent financial backlash entered into business legend.

It's not surprising then that for those who can afford it, and especially for political and business leaders who need to balance popularity with public image, the value of a speech writer who can craft a couple of well-chosen and appropriate one-liners is immeasurable.

For example, US President Barack Obama's 2011 speech at the annual White House Correspondents Dinner in Washington became a major hit on YouTube almost as soon as it was delivered and is, in effect, a well-written and well-delivered comedy routine. A YouTube search of top corporate speakers and sales presentations will also return many more examples of gags and one-liners, designed sometimes just to warm up the audience and sometimes to communicate important points in subtle and memorable ways.

While not every comedy writer will reach the heady heights of writing for world leaders, there are quite a few professional scriptwriters who make a very good living writing exclusively for the corporate market. Some of the skills needed for this kind of work are useful to every comedy writer, such as the ability to adapt and link jokes to a particular topic and, even more crucially, to produce material that is tailored to the strengths and avoids the weaknesses of speakers who may be accomplished in their own fields, but may not always share Obama's gifts as a public speaker. A key skill for speech writing that may not come quite so easily to all writers is the art of understanding the underlying message of the speaker well enough in the first place so that, unlike the Ratner incident mentioned earlier, the comedy element reinforces rather than works against the overall theme of the speech being delivered.

Theatre, film and novel writing

I have grouped these markets together for two reasons: firstly because they are certainly fields in which good comedy writing can lead to fame and fortune and secondly because, even when plays, movies and novels have a very comedic theme, there are usually skills over and above basic comedy writing ones needed to produce them. Long-running and much-revived farces by the likes of Ray Cooney or satirical hits like Yasmina Reza's *Art* or Bruce Norris's *Clybourne Park* may well have the critics raving about 'hilarious dialogue' and 'side-splitting plots' but in almost every case the writer has taken the time to develop a strong grasp of, and track record in, writing for theatre on a regular basis before hitting the big time.

Similarly, comedy writers have certainly been responsible for the scripts of funny and successful movies down through the years, from Neil Simon's *The Odd Couple* to Pegg and Frost's *Shaun of the Dead* and *Hot Fuzz* movies, to the works of Woody Allen, but again very few commercial movie projects are handed to first-time writers who have no previous track record. As for humour writing in book form, *Bridget Jones's Diary* or *A Year in Provence* may have caused commuters all over the world to laugh out loud on their journey to work, but the journey for the writers has normally been a somewhat longer one, involving establishing themselves in other fields of writing first. To take the two examples quoted above, journalism was the launch pad in Helen Fielding's case and copywriting in Peter Mayle's.

Having said all of that, there are still ways into all of these markets if you are really serious about them.

You can sign up for part-time or even full-time courses in play writing, screen writing and novel writing at many colleges and adult education centres. There is also a range of companion books by the publishers of this book which cover each of these writing disciplines in detail. In addition to learning the ropes, there are also practical steps you can take to break into each of these fields on a smaller scale. There are many small theatre companies, festivals and playwriting competitions which are open to new writers. There is also a thriving independent film-making scene to explore, fuelled by very little money but by large amounts of passion and commitment from volunteers working behind and in front of the cameras.

As for publishing, the days when self-publishing was seen as the last resort of the desperate writer are long gone. Thanks to sites like www.lulu.com it is now perfectly possible and legitimate for writers to upload their own fiction and non-fiction books online and have them sold to the public on a 'print on demand' basis.

Several recent humour bestsellers such as Stephen Clarke's *A Year in the Merde* first became hits in the online world to the extent that mainstream publishers were then encouraged to republish them as conventional books.

While you are working on your long-term writing projects, you might also consider honing your writing skills by turning your hand to journalistic pursuits. As you'll see from our next section this is another area where there are a lot of possibilities beyond the obvious and high-profile ones.

Journalism

Just as television eats up comedy ideas, several rainforests' worth of newspapers and magazines are churned out by the print industry every day of the week to inform, delight and fascinate and ultimately to end up lining cat litter trays. In the midst of all the hard and often depressing news there is often a market for good humorous writing and surprisingly few writers who can produce consistently good material to fill it. As with all of the media we are discussing in this chapter, the world of print journalism is changing rapidly and it is still somewhat difficult to predict exactly how the market will evolve in the coming years. One thing is certainly clear – the printed press has already lost the battle with twenty-four-hour TV, the internet and social media in terms of being first with the news. World events may move at the same speed they have always done, but the technological advances which make it possible for a news story from the most remote part of the globe to instantly appear on TV, computer and smartphone screens all over the world means that whatever headline is on today's newspaper is old news almost before it is printed.

With this in mind, publishers are looking at two responses – firstly, running websites alongside their paper publications, and secondly, finding selling points for the print editions that offer something other than speed of reporting. Both these challenges offer opportunities for the comedy writer. If a paper can no longer be first with the news, it may well be how well it analyses, discusses or presents an unusual angle on the news that attracts readers. And if papers are now competing with other internet providers in getting content online as fast as possible, a writer who can quickly produce consistently relevant and humorous material on any given topic may well be in demand.

The humorous column has been a long-standing feature of newspapers dating back to the time when they were the one and only mass medium, and the work of the best writers in this style from previous eras such as Alan Coren or Erma Bombeck can still be read with enjoyment today. Many of today's columns are headlined by current celebrities and it is probably not shattering many illusions to point out that a sizeable number of these columns are ghostwritten on behalf of whichever famous face appears in the picture at the top. If you have a talent for punchy, topical writing in somebody else's style and are not too concerned about getting any credit for your work, there may well be some harassed PR person only too pleased to hear from you.

A good exercise would be to keep an eye on the newer reality shows or the up-and-coming soap actors, and try to identify in advance who might become the 'nation's favourite' in six months or so. The time to approach their management with your suggested sample column is now so they can pitch it to the papers as part of their image-building campaign. (Speed counts here – by the time they are famous enough that the papers are approaching them, there will already be a journalist or existing writer assigned to the job.)

The mainstream magazine market is another area where humour articles can find a niche. General interest publications for both sexes such as *Cosmopolitan*, *FHM* and *GQ* will usually have regular humour columns (often on the last page). Most non celebrity-fronted regular columns are awarded to writers who have caught the editor and the readership's imagination with a consistent supply of good one-off articles over a period of time, so this may be the best approach to take at first.

Special interest publications such as *Men's Health* or one of the sports titles are also good to explore, particularly if you have an actual interest in the topic and can write something funny about it that also communicates that you know what you are talking about.

Although some humour which works in print will not work live, and vice versa, many of the ideas you have generated for your scripted comedy will work just as well in article form if presented properly. As I write I have in front of me a copy of *New Woman* magazine which has an illustrated article about the horrible dances men do in nightclubs. The article could just as easily be the basis for a stand-up comedy routine or a TV sketch – indeed it may well have become one by the time you read this.

If you are a male writer, women's magazines are often in the market for ironic pieces which explain how the male brain works (or doesn't), and men's magazines are just as keen on women's views on more or less the same topic as long as you can write them in the appropriate flirty/vampy tone that suits the magazine you are pitching to.

Another standard feature of magazine humour is the 'list'-type feature or tongue-in-cheek quiz – '100 ways to dump your boyfriend', 'Ten things not to say on your first date', 'Are you a sad seventies throwback?', etc. If you can come up with new comedy slants on basic relationship and lifestyle topics, you'll find you have a lot of saleable magazine-type features.

A smaller scale way of getting your comedy into print and actually getting paid for it is to keep an eye out for letters pages in newspapers and magazines which offer payment for the best letter or, even better, for every letter published. The winning letters often offer a clever or ironic take on a previous issue's article. Although the prize amounts aren't huge there is nothing to stop you writing to a number of publications on a regular basis.

On the more intellectual end of the scale, you may wish to exercise your talents and your competitive nature all at once by entering the literary competitions run by 'upmarket' publications which often delight in setting tasks for readers ranging from 'Write a poem in honour of the newest iPhone' to 'Compose a sales pitch for a home-based nuclear waste dump'. These competitions have their regular entrants and submissions are often of extremely high quality. The prizes are usually token at best, but the opportunity to stretch your creative brain is often of far more value.

Comedy writing for children

Children have always enjoyed humour and both the children's broadcast and print markets are very open to humorous writing, whether it is out-and-out comedy or comedy applied to educational and informative topics to make them more palatable. One of the most successful book series of the past decade has been Terry Deary's *Horrible Histories* books which put an irreverent spin on different historical eras ranging from *The Vicious Vikings* to *The Vile Victorians* but with the humour all solidly based on fact. The books have subsequently been adapted into a TV series, a live theatrical show and a wide range of other merchandising avenues. Humour is particularly attractive to publishers trying to reach the notoriously reluctant 'boy reader' and series like *Captain Underpants* and *Diary of a Wimpy Kid* have combined cartoon drawings with broad humour to bridge that gap. Girls haven't done too badly in the humour stakes either, with writers like Louise Rennison and Carolyn Mackler producing hugely popular books (which boys secretly read too!).

Despite all the new and exciting writers and concepts which blossom in the children's market each season, more traditional joke and novelty books also remain strong sellers, much to the dismay of teachers and parents who have to listen to the same jokes over and over again. A particular skill which is relevant to all comedy writing but particularly to writing for children is to know your audience very well. What a seven-year-old understands and finds funny may be very different from what a twelve-year-old likes.

Much humour writing is based on wordplay, but in order to appreciate even a simple joke like 'What's brown and sticky?' and the answer ('A stick'), the listener not only needs to understand the words 'brown', 'sticky' and 'stick', but also has to catch on to the connection between the words 'stick' and 'sticky'. What's more, they need to be familiar with the idea that what makes this joke funny is that the answer is the obvious one rather than the usual 'clever' one more commonly found in jokes.

While the average nine-year-old would be familiar enough with all these concepts to find this kind of joke funny, four- or five-year-olds, who are just learning the rules of language but haven't got round to learning the rules of jokes yet, may just be confused.

Market-testing your writing on children from the age group you are aiming at is not just helpful but essential. Besides the fact that 'What age group are you aiming at?' is one of the first questions any producer or publisher is likely to throw at you, the feedback from a young reader is likely to be one of the most honest you will ever get – whether or not it is the feedback you actually wanted!

The same 'knowing your audience' principle is essential when aiming your scripted comedy at children in a TV or theatrical setting. Certainly any writer whose main reason for targeting the children's market is that it seems an easier one to break into than the adult market is in for a shock. If anything, writing or performing comedy for children and holding their attention, let alone making them laugh, can be a lot harder than it is with adults – if you don't believe me, ask any harassed children's party entertainer.

There is certainly a lot of marketing money invested in children's entertainment but for this reason the standard of work required can be a lot higher too. The most lighthearted children's show or publication has usually been tested rigorously to check that it meets various legal, educational and age-level-appropriate requirements before it hits the market.

To save yourself a lot of fruitless effort, taking time to talk to children, teachers, booksellers, theatre managers and (if you can get to them) programme makers is a very important first step in getting familiar with what is needed, what is allowed and what is possible in this market.

One other element to bear in mind when designing projects for the children's market, in particular book and TV projects, is the all-important appeal of the franchise. While one-off projects by new writers may be of interest to producers and publishers they are much more likely to be interested if they can see that an idea has 'series potential'.

One phenomenon with young audiences that will probably never change is the fact that once children approach pre-teen years they tend not to want to watch shows aimed at their own age group and instead want to watch what they think the older, cooler kids are watching. A writer who can give scripts the feeling of having a slightly rude or dangerous edge to please the kids, while at the same time keeping the content safely within the bounds of what parents and programme watchdogs are happy for them to actually watch, can do very well in this market.

Advertising

From *Rising Damp* star Leonard Rossiter spilling his drink over Joan Collins, to Rowan Atkinson's incompetent secret agent who refused to carry a credit card, to the Budweiser Frogs and their 'Whasssup?' catchphrase, many TV and cinema ads feature top comedy performers and excellent comedy writing and in some cases have bigger budgets and higher production values than many TV shows and movies. In the case of Atkinson's secret agent, the character was so popular that years later it evolved into the hero of the *Johnny English* movie franchise.

If you frequently find yourself thinking 'I could have written that' when you see the latest comedy-based TV or press advertising campaign, there are two options that you may wish to consider, neither of which will instantly gain you access to a *Mad Men* style world of big contracts and glamorous overseas shoots but which are certainly worth considering if you feel your talents may lie in this direction.

The first is to explore the world of copywriting which, when you start out, is likely to involve writing about far less interesting subjects than those usually advertised on the small or silver screens. It is also going to require you to get some kind of marketing or sales-related qualification if you don't already have one. Like it or not, the world of advertising has its rules and conventions which are as firm and widespread as the entertainment industry, and the appropriate qualification is often the only way into the top firms. While you may understandably feel that talent should be enough, advertising is a competitive industry and there are plenty of people out there with talent who also have a degree.

The other, less formal, route involves doing some research and working out which production companies actually made the ads that have caught your attention, and sending them samples of your writing so they can bear you in mind for further projects. You will usually find that writers on the bigger budget commercials are, more often than not, the same top-ranked professionals who work on the regular programmes, so unless your work is of equivalent quality or you have a reasonable number of credits to your own name, don't be too surprised if you aren't first on the list to be called when their next job comes in. However, if you make a very good presentation you may get some useful feedback and perhaps even some suggestions about how best to take your own 'advertising campaign' forward in terms of securing work.

To actually get your advertising talents used more quickly, you may want to set your sights a little lower. Is there a local business advertising on radio or in the local press for which you could come up with a better campaign? The financial return may not be huge and you will need to approach prospective customers sensitively – nobody likes to be told their ads are rubbish even if they secretly know that they are – but in this way, in return for a little time and effort, you might be able to kick-start the building of your advertising portfolio.

T-shirts, bumper stickers...

'My uncle/brother/mum went to London/New York/Rio and all I got was this lousy T-shirt', 'I'm with stupid', 'Stupid's with me', 'Honk if you're horny', 'My other car's a Porsche'. Yes, I know you have probably seen and heard them all before, but that's because a clever T-shirt slogan or bumper sticker is likely to get reproduced, ripped off and reused for years and years. People are always on the lookout for new ones though, and if you are good at coming up with topical ideas and can get into the market early you might actually make some money before the rip-off merchants get to work.

Not too long ago, the only way of doing this was either by investing your own cash in purchasing the shirts, mugs or whatever other item you were planning to sell, getting them printed up as cheaply as you could and then hitting the streets while they still had novelty value. Alternatively, you could try to persuade your local printing shop to partner you in your comedy enterprise. Either method still can and does pay off with the right slogan at the right time, but the internet now also offers a wide range of 'print on demand' sites which allow you to upload your slogan on a wide range of products which will only get printed and dispatched when somebody actually buys one.

It's certainly worth a try next time that killer slogan pops into your head. Of course, in mentioning this market here, I am not so much suggesting you focus your entire comedy writing career on decorating T-shirts and mugs as pointing out that no matter how much the comedy writing market develops and continues to change, there will always be opportunities for you to use your comedy writing skills if you are prepared to look for them, target them and continue pursuing them. As you continue to explore the suggested markets in this chapter (no doubt there will be many other markets you can think of that I have left out), perhaps the best way for you to decide which area to focus on is to try several on a small scale, to see which give you the best results.

As comedy skills develop over time, none of this practice will be wasted. Even if you are strongly drawn to one area such as sitcom, studying how stand-up routines are put together will give you useful practice in blending dialogue and character. Whatever type of comedy you set your sights on, there is one basic building block you will need to have a constant supply of: jokes, jokes and more jokes. In the next chapter we will learn how to create them.

Over to you . . .

Just as learning to write comedy means looking beyond the surface of particular types of humour to see what 'makes them tick', making headway in any particular writing market requires getting to know that market very well from both an artistic and a business point of view.

Whichever market or markets you are interested in targeting, set yourself the goal of becoming as knowledgeable in that field as you can. This will involve allocating time and focus rather than just skimming the surface. If you want to work in television or radio, you need to set aside time to watch and listen to as many shows of the type you want to target as you can. If you aim to work in theatre or film you need to attend the latest plays and movies regularly. If humour writing, whether fiction or non-fiction, is your game, you need to read as many current examples of successful writing as you can.

Most of all you'll need to know what's going on behind the scenes and between the lines. Who are the up-and-coming writers making a name for themselves in the markets you are aiming for yourself? What is it about their work that is working so well for them? What can you learn from what they are doing either in their writing or in their career path that you can apply to your own work? Which trade and industry publications, websites and blogs do you need to be reading regularly to find out this kind of information? Are there local theatre or film festivals, writers' groups or other networks you can tap into to increase your market knowledge?

The resource section at the end of this book should help with some of the above questions, but the most effective research is usually the research you do for yourself and the sooner you start this aspect of building your writing career the better.

3

Basic Joke Writing

Probably the most common question asked of professional humorists is 'Where do you get your ideas from?' I know it's the most common question I get asked – in fact I'm usually the one asking it, whenever I'm staring at a blank screen with a splitting headache, butterflies in my stomach and a deadline just around the corner.

My most intense experience of deadline pressure was some years ago when I was lead writer for a morning radio show which was three hours long and went on the air at 6 a.m., five days a week. Even though a lot of the airtime was filled with music, commercials and reports on news, traffic and weather, it still meant a quota of at least fifty new gags needed every morning to get us safely to 9 o'clock. As I was working on this particular show at a time when the widespread use of the internet was still a few years away, those fifty gags needed to come from my brain rather than from cyberspace.

I'm not a night person, and the nature of topical humour is that it can't be written very far in advance, so I would usually find myself groping my way out of bed at around 4 a.m. to grab a quick look at the early editions of the morning newspapers (no internet, remember?) and then launch into a hectic session of joke writing as the programme's start time loomed like an oncoming express.

Was it hard? Yes. Was it as hard as it sounds at first? No.

Much as I'd love to create the picture of myself as the Indiana Jones of the comedy writing world, snatching each morning show from the jaws of doom, comedy writing is like any other profession: the longer you practise the more efficient you get, and along the way you pick up various handy techniques and tricks of the trade which allow you to do a good job even under pressure.

In this chapter I'm going to try to pass on some of the tips and tricks I've personally picked up which help me get jobs like that one done on time. As there's no set course of study or standard qualification for being a comedy writer, there are no doubt other ways of generating humour which I haven't come across yet. But these are the ones that work for me and I'm pretty sure that if you follow the same process, by the time you reach the end of this chapter, you'll also be able to come up with workable jokes whenever you need to.

Whether you'll still want to is a different matter entirely. There's no magic to the joke-writing process. It's basically a step-by-step method of analysing existing joke structures that have worked for other people and then applying the same structures to your own ideas. To do this requires investing a significant amount of concentrated effort – especially when you are new to the process.

From the point of view of teaching comedy, the process of breaking down humour into its component parts has been compared to dissecting a frog – in the process, the frog dies. So please bear in mind as you read through the following pages that setting out the basic steps in printed form will tend to stretch out a process which in your own brain you'll soon learn to do a lot faster. Having gone through the basic steps as laid out here, the only way to really make it work for you is to try it out on your own ideas. Of course, for some people, getting any ideas at all is the hard part so let's get that problem out of the way first.

Beating the blank page

Different comedians have different ideas about what constitutes the world's worst comedic experience. For some it's trying to perform to a drunken, baying mob at a stag night, hen party or corporate function when the audience has difficulty seeing straight never mind listening to your gems of polished wit. For others it's playing to an audience exclusively made up of critics and reviewers or, worst of all, other comedians – the kind who don't laugh at anyone else's jokes because they are too professional, too cool or more likely just plain jealous. Then there are the gigs every comic experiences at some time or other, where no matter what you do the jokes just don't work and you either get booed offstage or walk off to total silence except for the sound of your own feet.

But whatever the individual comedian's particular bugbear may be, the chances are they will come up against it only occasionally and as their career progresses they may eventually be able to avoid less attractive gigs altogether.

For almost every comedy writer, there is no question as to what the 'world's worst feeling' is – that fatal combination of a deadline and an empty sheet of paper or Word document staring back at you. No matter how good you get, or how successful your career becomes, it's an experience that can never be totally avoided.

Let's not be overdramatic about this. Sometimes coming up with the comedy goods isn't so hard at all. You're in a good mood, you're confident in your supreme funniness, flashes of inspiration light up your brain like an electrical storm and golden shafts of wit flow off the end of your pen or bounce off your keyboard almost faster than you can jot them down. I wish you many, many days like that in your writing career.

But if you're anything like the rest of us, you're likely to have the other kind of comedy writing day too – the one when the only thing blanker than your writing surface is your brain. Maybe you've got pressing bills to pay, a hangover, a sick child, other things on your mind. Maybe it's your first big job or your first time working for a new client whom you've already told how good you are and now you are under pressure to prove it. Or maybe you are just not in the mood to be funny today.

Well, maybe this is when we find out if you really have what it takes to be a professional comedy writer or if you're just somebody who can think up something funny once in a while when you happen to feel like it.

Fortunately, there are some emergency techniques for times like this. And here is one of the most useful ones.

How to kick-start your comedy brain

As we have already noted, the joke-writing process is a very basic one and it starts with the most basic question of all: 'What exactly do I want to write jokes about?'

Comedy has been described as one of the few professions in the world where as soon as you tell people what you do for a living they immediately want you to prove it. 'So you're a comedy writer? Go on then – tell us a joke.'

Surely that should be the easiest thing in the world if you already do it for a living and all the easier for us comedy writers who can create jokes from scratch? Except that it isn't. Because before you tell a joke, you need to know what kind of joke is required. A long joke, a short joke, a 'knock, knock' joke, a joke about chickens . . . Now, if you were asked for a joke about chickens you could very quickly run through your mental filing cabinet of jokes about chickens and select the poultry-related joke most likely to knock the assembled audience dead. Even if you don't happen to know any chicken jokes, maybe you have heard one about a duck that you can retell, changing the lead character to a chicken just for this particular evening. Failing that, there must be a joke about some member of the animal kingdom which could be adapted – for example, you could change the crocodile who walked into the bar in that joke we used in Chapter One into a chicken, and the joke would still work.

My point here is that 'Tell us a joke' is such a general request that it actually gets more difficult the more jokes you have to choose from. But once you have a subject to work on, your brain can start the process of sorting and combining ideas that leads to the production of humour.

The reason I'm labouring this point a bit is simply because I have seen so many would-be comedy writers driving themselves crazy trying to come up with 'jokes' when if they started off by giving themselves a list of topics and then concentrated on coming up with jokes for each topic, they could focus their minds a lot more easily.

I've always been slightly bemused by writers who find the idea of writing topical gags more daunting than writing other kinds of joke. Yes, I know the tighter deadline can be a little more scary, but at least you can spend less time racking your brains and get on with the actual joke writing.

Speaking of joke writing, just a few words in defence of the humble 'joke', 'gag', 'one-liner' or 'quip' from a comedy writing point of view. An American writing colleague recently suggested that the most important question a comedy writer needs to ask is not the 'What am I trying to write jokes about?' one we are discussing here, but 'What am I trying to write *comedy* about?' This stems from the idea that modern comedy is less about the kind of 'mechanical' jokes beloved of more old-fashioned music hall and vaudeville-style comedians and much more about the emotions, point of view and attitude of the comedian or writer. I absolutely agree with this from an artistic perspective and we will be talking about this approach when we look at comedy routines in the next chapter. However, from the point of view of a working comedy writer I think the ability to understand and write jokes is as important today as it has ever been. It's a bit like the necessity of knowing basic notes and chord structures for musicians. Even if those musicians are jazz improvisers and intend to take the music off in new, unheard of and highly personal directions, there has to be an underlying structure to start from.

It is certainly the comedian or comedy writer's unique 'take' on the world which makes their work not only funny but individual and memorable, but this perspective has to be communicated to the audience in a way that makes them laugh, and more often than not the best way to deliver comic ideas with the widest impact is to apply proven and time-tested joke structures. Listen closely to even the most modern, personal and 'stream of consciousness' style comics and you will start to spot the same underlying joke structures and comedy techniques that comics and jesters have been using for centuries.

As a professional comedy writer, a unique and personal approach to your work is certainly something worth developing. However, being a professional as well as an artist means that you won't necessarily always be producing work on topics you personally have strong feelings about. This is yet another reason why you will find basic joke structures useful for keeping you productive and on track whatever the brief you are working to.

All of which brings us back to our current battle with that blank page. And there it is, still staring straight back at us, mocking us, daring us to be funny. So let's break the deadlock by doing something the little bully doesn't expect: let's try *not* to be funny.

If you're not already familiar with the concept of brainstorming, I won't blame you if your instinct is to leave us at this point. ('Try not to be funny? Now *there's* a really useful comedy writing technique!') But trust me a little longer and I'll try to explain.

Of course we will need to end up with something funny eventually, but if jokes are the basic building blocks of that funny end product then in order to create those building blocks we need to first get busy with straw, mud and water. In comedy writing terms the raw material for our 'building bricks' is words and ideas. So what we need to do first is brainstorm all of the words and ideas that a particular joke topic suggests.

Let's see how this works by applying it to a typical topical press clipping of the sort that pops up in newspapers or on news websites every day:

> Romantic Pete Robbins has had a picture of his wedding day tattooed on his leg. The tattoo shows Pete in a dark suit along with his wife Sandy in her wedding dress and the date of their marriage last month. Pete, 24, said 'It was painful but well worth it.'

Oh yes, this is the kind of heady stuff that takes me right back to the days of live breakfast radio. Some days we'd write ground-breaking satirical comedy on major historic events . . . other days we'd have to make do with Pete and his tattooed thigh. But whatever story or topic we're working on, our next task remains the same: to open our minds to every possible thought, word and idea we can associate with that topic.

Obviously there are lots of words and images associated with weddings – bells, bridesmaids, ministers, families, family quarrels, the best man (who usually loses the ring), movies like *Four Weddings and a Funeral* or *My Big Fat Greek Wedding*, wedding day nerves – we keep going until we have exhausted all the possibilities. Then there are all those wedding-related phrases and sayings : 'Happy ever after', 'If anyone knows a reason why these two should not be joined together . . .', 'Something old, something new, something borrowed, something blue'.

You can collect all these words and images in your head, but it's usually much more useful to jot them down on a sheet of paper or make lists on your computer screen. As you can see, we're not concerned at the moment about what is or isn't funny, we just want to collect as much material as possible for our joke-writing later on. The other key element of the news story we have chosen is the tattoo, so we need to think about all the images and items we associate with tattoos. There are needles and tattoo parlours. There are the kinds of images often used for tattoos such as flowers, daggers, or words like 'Mum'. There are the kinds of people we associate with tattoos. Just as we are not concerning ourselves with what is or isn't funny at this point, this isn't the time to edit or censor our ideas either. I must confess that when I think of tattoos I still inevitably think of wrestlers, pirates and tough guys because those were usually the kinds of people who had them when I was growing up. These days tattoos are much more mainstream, with many models and pop stars sporting them as fashion statements. Nevertheless, whatever images and ideas the word 'tattoo' sparks for me have a right to go on my list just as if your great-grandmother happens to have tattoos she deserves a place on your list even if nobody else would associate great-grandmothers with tattoos.

Next on the list come all the more tangential things we might associate with weddings and tattoos – for instance, weddings are celebrations, so we might decide to list other kinds of celebrations such as birthdays, christenings, anniversaries. Body piercings and tattoos often go together. A tattoo parlour is a place you go to change your look, as is a barber's, a manicurist's, a cosmetic surgery – the list can go on for as long as you like.

As you work on your list look for opposite associations as well as things that are similar. For instance, weddings might remind you of funerals. By the way, in making my own list I've just realised how strongly my Irish Catholic upbringing has influenced my visualising of this story – so far I've been picturing the wedding as taking place in a church, but of course it could just as easily take place in a registry office, or on a Caribbean island, or as a themed wedding in a zoo or a museum. As each new possibility strikes me, it is added to my list. Right now the list might seem very random and not particularly amusing but at least I'm not looking at a blank page any more. And if I start to take ideas from one part of the list and add them to ideas from another, there is at last a chance I might (even accidentally) generate something that resembles a joke.

If you are already good at ad-libbing jokes you may feel that the whole brainstorming process seems a bit tedious and unnecessary, but one of its big advantages is that not only does it help you produce jokes, it helps you come up with less obvious ones.

So even if you do have one of those 'golden days' when jokes pop out of your brain without much effort, it is still worth running through the more methodical system suggested here just in case it throws up some others that don't spring to mind quite as easily. After all, if something springs to your mind too easily there is a good chance it has sprung to other minds too.

Whenever a celebrity football player is the subject of a sexual scandal (which seems to happen these days with almost the same frequency as the regular match fixtures) it's not difficult to come up with jokes based on stock football phrases such as 'scoring' and 'playing away from home' without too much thought. The trouble is that every other comedy writer, tweeter and bar room drunk in town is likely to come up with exactly the same jokes. This even applies to 'new' jokes. As I was writing this chapter I heard a news report that legendary British comic and TV presenter Bruce Forsyth, famous for decades in Britain for his catchphrase 'Nice to see you, to see you nice!', had finally been knighted by the Queen at the age of eighty-three. The clever line 'Knight to see you, to see you Knight' immediately popped into my head as no doubt it did into yours before you even read my version.

You won't be surprised to hear that the quick internet search I made just an hour after hearing that news announcement already displayed 230 separate headlines, tweets and blogs using exactly the same gag. I am sure there will be quite a few more by now, should you wish to do your own search, but I doubt that any of the original 230 people (or 231 if you include me) who wrote it on the day the story first broke copied it from anyone else. It is just a case of the first line that springs to mind not always being the most unique one.

The danger of too much duplication is even more the case with perennial topics like marriage, politics, growing up – subjects on which countless jokes and routines have already been written. Certainly, when faced with one of these 'same old subjects' yet again, you can take the easy way out and either recycle or slightly upgrade the same old jokes you wrote last time. And to be honest, when faced with a very pressing deadline it is something most of us have had to do at some point or other. But if you are working to make a name for yourself in this competitive comedy business, you'll want to develop a reputation for creating fresh, original, funny ideas – for writing the jokes that only you can write. Brainstorming, with all its wild tangents and potential to create and connect seemingly unrelated ideas, greatly increases the chances of your being able to do this.

Now let's start combining some of the ideas our tattoo story generated and see what we can come up with.

Finding the right combination

Looking over the list of associations I made with 'weddings' I notice the word 'minister', which starts me wondering if the groom was the only one at the wedding who had a tattoo:

> Have you heard about the groom who had his wedding picture tattooed on his leg? He said the pain was terrible but he still managed to read out his marriage vows clearly.
>
> Because the minister had them tattooed on his forehead.

You'll note that the resulting joke is only loosely related to the original clipping (presumably the wedding picture was tattooed on Pete's leg after the ceremony, not before). It's also quite wordy and contrived. But just as we are not worried about quality control when it comes to getting words and ideas down on our lists in the first place, now isn't the time to exercise quality control in relation to the jokes we are constructing from them. In the second stage of the process we just want to come up with as many jokes as we can, as quickly as we can. We can be selective later.

Let's try another combination. We noted that in many wedding-day stories the best man loses the ring and I also mentioned that tattoos made me think of the related subject of body piercing. Put these two ideas together and you might end up with something like this:

> Two body piercers got married but they had trouble exchanging the rings.
>
> They were still attached to the best man's navel.

To add to the various laughter theories mentioned in the first chapter, some scientists believe that the laughter reaction is triggered when our brain is forced to entertain two incongruous ideas at the same time. On the one hand there's the fairly staid image of a very traditional wedding ceremony with marriage vows and the exchanging of rings. Then we combine it with the more unusual imagery of a church minister with letters tattooed across his forehead or of the bride and groom trying to put on rings which are still attached to the best man. Our brain has trouble juggling these two ideas at the same time, tension builds up, and then we have to laugh to relieve that tension. Well, that's how the theory goes.

All I know for sure is that combining ideas like this often leads to usable joke material even when there is very little comedy in the original source material. Of course not every individual combination will work, so the process will also throw up lots of unworkable jokes and unusable material. If that happens just move on to the next item on your list. Remember our task at this point is still primarily not 'being funny' – it is simply to put the ideas we have generated together in as many combinations as we can. Put enough of them together and ideas which are funny will inevitably start to emerge – sometimes very far removed from what triggered the ideas in the first place:

Heard about the body piercer who tried to commit bigamy?

The minister saw right through him.

To boldly go where lots of people have gone before

The more you practise combining ideas, the easier moulding them into jokes will get. But 'easier' isn't quite the same thing as 'easy'. So are there other techniques we can use to help us generate jokes? Yes there are – the same techniques and joke formulas that comedy writers have been using for centuries.

Just as drama writers sometimes argue that from *Romeo and Juliet* to *Casablanca* there are only about seven basic plots, comedy writers often debate how many original joke formulas actually exist. No two people seem to agree on the exact number but most writers agree that the number of original joke formulas is very small, with every other joke being just a variation on the original few.

The 'riddle', one of the oldest forms of joke, has been traced back over many thousands of years. In fact one of the earliest recorded versions, written in Old English still turns up in children's joke books today, loosely translated as 'How many pieces of leather would it take to reach the moon? One, if it be long enough.' The joke below goes back even further – to the fourth or fifth century AD, it is believed – and is one most of us will have heard before in its almost identical modern version:

> Asked by the court barber how he wanted his hair cut, the king replied: 'In silence.'

Children in particular are very fond of formula jokes, ranging from 'knock, knock' jokes to pupil–teacher exchanges which work to exactly the same formula as the barber joke above.

> Teacher: How do you like school?
>
> Pupil: Closed.

'Lightbulb' jokes are formulaic jokes which appeal to adults and children alike, the only difference being the subject matter.

> How many teachers does it take to screw in a lightbulb?
>
> Two. One to screw the lightbulb in and one to make him do it over and over again till he gets it right.

> How many bankers does it take to screw in a lightbulb?
>
> None. Bankers are much too busy screwing the rest of us.

As it might be a bit difficult to build a mainstream comedy career based on 'knock, knock' and 'lightbulb' jokes, let's take a look at a few slightly more serviceable joke types you can try using in your own work.

Literal meanings and multiple meanings

One of the most confusing things for people learning any language, but particularly English, is discovering the huge number of phrases in common use which sound like they mean one thing but in a different context, with a different inflection and sometimes with absolutely no rhyme or reason at all, suddenly turn out to mean something else. When we hear about someone 'talking through their hat', most of us know they are not actually speaking through their headgear but are in fact talking rubbish. (And in using the phrase 'talking rubbish' I'm assuming you'll know that I don't mean the person in question is spewing garbage out of their mouth.)

'I'm going to kill that husband of mine', 'Stop sitting on the fence', 'You've got the wrong end of the stick'. We are so used to understanding the implied meaning of phrases like this, that a very useful joke technique is simply to remind us how ridiculous it would be if we interpreted the words literally.

I've got one deaf ear.

I found it on the floor of a barbershop in Glasgow.

Online dating really worked for me.

I've just got engaged to an iPhone.

Along with phrases which seem to say one thing and actually mean another, a further pitfall for the English language learner is the fact that so many words have more than one meaning. But what is a challenge for the language student is a great boon to the joke writer.

My father's very worried about his blood test next week.

He's been up for the last three nights studying.

This is obviously a play on the fact that 'test', which means 'an investigation' in the medical context, can also mean an examination in the educational world. As well as being a romantic encounter in our 'online dating' example above, the word 'date' is also used to describe a fruit. This is the same basis on which the front of a cartoon greetings card can promise: 'For your birthday I've set you up with a hot date' and once opened display the punchline: 'but he couldn't make it so you'll have to settle for this sunburned raisin instead' with a cartoon version of the aforementioned fruit winking at the recipient.

I could give many more examples, as I am sure you also could. In fact, when I think about it, I'm tempted to revise my earlier statement – in English it's not just many words that have a number of different meanings, it's almost *every* word if you look hard enough. In some cases just one word can have a whole range of different meanings. The word 'range' itself is a good example. It can mean a variety of things ('a wide range of products'), it can relate to distance ('long range'), it can be used as a verb ('to range far and wide'), it can be a place ('home on the range'). And we haven't even begun to discuss the many words which aren't 'range' but, at least in the service of a joke, can be made to sound very similar:

Tonto went into the bank to get a mortgage.

They told him he'd have to discuss it with the Loan Arranger.

Some of the most useful words in a comedy writer's dictionary are the small, innocent words like 'for' or 'on' which have different meanings depending on what context they are used in. Fool the listener into thinking they are being used in one way and you can create a joke by using them in another.

I wanted to get a dog for my husband

but the people in the pet store said they don't do swaps.

The joke hinges on the fact that 'for' can mean 'doing something on somebody's behalf' but can also be used to mean that something (or in this case somebody) has been exchanged or traded in place of something else. The joke only works if we make sure the set-up line fools the listener into thinking we are using the former meaning when in fact we are using the latter. To do this we use 'for' in the context of a very familiar phrase – we are all used to hearing about people buying presents 'for' other people, to the point where we don't think about any other possible meanings. That's why the second line, revealing that 'for' was being used in an entirely different way, surprises us and triggers the laugh. (Or at least it might have done before my explaining the joke in such detail killed it!) Note that in the set-up line to this joke the woman didn't say 'I wanted to *buy* a dog for my husband.' We may have assumed 'get a dog' would involve buying one – in fact that's what we were intended to assume – but the word 'get' was used very deliberately so that the 'swapping' or 'trading' idea in the second line would work.

Amateur joke tellers often mess up a gag by accidentally using the wrong word in their set-up line, and either giving away the punchline or changing the set-up, so that when the punchline is revealed it doesn't 'work' with what has gone before. Professional comedy writers display their professionalism once they have their basic joke ideas by going over them again and again, and refining them so that they are the right combination of the right words in the right amount to achieve the maximum comedy effect.

Here's another example using the word 'on':

For our tenth anniversary I took my wife across Europe on the Orient Express.

By our twenty-fifth anniversary I might be earning enough for us to travel inside it.

Again, it's the scene-setting in the first line that lulls us into thinking we know what's going on. Notice that in the second line we don't say in so many words that the happy couple were clinging to the outside of the train – we let the audience create that image for themselves. That way they can laugh not only at the surprise but also at their own cleverness in working it out.

Even when we do know what context a word is being used in, we can still be fooled:

'Do you believe in sex before marriage?'

'Not if it keeps the guests waiting.'

In this case we were quite right in thinking that 'before' meant 'in advance of' – we just didn't know how far in advance was being suggested until the second line lets us know we are talking about moments rather than the months or years we might at first have assumed.

You may have spotted that this joke works in exactly the same way as the 'peeing in the swimming pool' example we used in Chapter One. Here's how a similar joke might work with the tattoo story in our current example:

'My brother's wedding was called off because the bride got a tattoo.'

'But these days lots of women get tattoos.'

'Not halfway through the ceremony'.

Obviously the number of words and phrases which allow possibilities for comedy wordplay could fill several books, and practising with and discovering all the possible multiple meanings and variations should be an ongoing process throughout the comedy writer's career. There is of course one form of wordplay which you don't have to be a comedy writer or need much practice to be an expert at . . .

Double entendres

Even in the modern era, where almost anything can be said out loud and directly, euphemism and double entendre are still very popular joke devices. Named after the French phrase for 'double meaning', the more general understanding is that a double entendre's other meaning is what the *Oxford English Dictionary* delicately describes as an 'indelicate' one. Certainly there are many words in the English language that can be given a suggestive connotation: jerk, screw, tool, sausage, hump – the list can go on forever and in some comedy acts often does.

Most overworked of all is the little word 'it' which is frequently used to stand in for a sexual act:

Comedians do it standing up.

Dancers do it to music.

Comedy writers brainstorm before they do it.

'Excuse me, ma'am, I have a letter for you.'

'Can you come upstairs and give it to me?'

'Sure – and would you like me to bring the letter too?'

While I would never deny that in an emergency any gag is better than no gag, the problem with comedy 'gems' like that last one is that they are so mechanical that even the slowest audience can work out the punchline before you get there.

But that's not to say double entendre can't be done elegantly. The classic Mae West line 'Is that a gun in your pocket or are you just pleased to see me?' combines a seemingly innocent enquiry with a not so innocent mental picture. It's almost a visual double entendre in that the audience has to visualise the scene and complete the picture for themselves to get the other meaning. A visual version of the same line was used in the Mel Brooks movie *Blazing Saddles* delivered by saloon singer Madeline Kahn to a cowboy watching the show with his hat in his lap. We hear her say, 'Is that a ten-gallon hat or are you just enjoying the show?' We look at the hat in the cowboy's lap and then we laugh because we 'get' what she is suggesting. A similar 'ping pong' effect happens in the double entendre joke below:

'I'd like to buy some deodorant, please.'

'The ball type?'

'No, it's for under my arms.'

In order to laugh at the punchline we have to cast our minds back to the second line, because the mention of 'arms' in the last line has alerted us that the 'ball' referred to in the second line could mean a part of the anatomy as well as a type of cosmetic bottle. Once again, note how the wording of what seems like a simple joke is crucial. If the second line was 'the type with a ball?' the double meaning in the third line wouldn't be possible.

A technique particularly favoured by classic British comedians such as Max Miller and Frankie Howerd and which still works well for comics who have a similar intimate rapport with their audiences (although it takes a lot of talent to genuinely develop that rapport), is to work lines into their routines which are blatantly of the double meaning sort – 'a man with a very large organ' is a frequent character in this kind of joke. The comic then waits for the audience to laugh, before looking shocked and telling them off for having such dirty minds. The resulting laugh is usually bigger than the one the suggestive line caused in the first place.

Like it or not, pushing the boundaries is an essential part of comedy. In fact it could be argued that if comedy isn't offending someone somewhere, it's probably so bland as to be completely ineffective. Whether you personally tend towards the 'whiter than white' or 'bluer than blue' end of that spectrum, you have every right to your own opinion. But from a work point of view it is worth considering both sides of the story.

This can work both ways. In his early career UK comic and actor Russell Brand had a reputation for very frank and sexually explicit material drawn from what, by his own admission, was an equally wild personal life at the time. While his unique combination of notoriety and undeniable charm had made him a popular figure on digital TV channels, it was taking part in mainstream shows such as the popular 'reality' series *Celebrity Big Brother* which really led to a career breakthrough. Hosting the live late-night round-up of the reality show's daily events, Brand was typically flamboyant and often very risqué, which might be taken as proof that when a performer or writer is talented they can push the boundaries as far as they like. However, Brand's agent at the time has since revealed that in order to get the channel's agreement to allow him on the air in the first place, guarantees had to be given that the agency would compensate the producers if he went too far 'over the top'. Most comedy writers wouldn't be able to make such a guarantee from their own resources or have an agent willing to back them to that extent, so no matter how wide the boundaries of what you are allowed to write depending on the pro-gramme you are working for, it makes sense to know what those boundaries are and stick to them if you want to keep working.

On the other end of the scale, it is not unusual for well-known TV comics to include material in their live DVDs which is more 'adult' than they would normally use. In some cases this is because their live act is genuinely edgier than their TV-orientated work, but it is also by no means unknown for the bluer material to be added specifically to the DVD script because market research has shown that the predominantly young male audience for stand-up DVDs is less likely to buy one which doesn't display an 'adults only' classification on the cover.

Backwards writing and blasts from the past

As we discussed at the beginning of this chapter, if you set your-selves the task of only coming up with great jokes, you run the risk of making the job so hard that you won't be able to come up with any jokes at all. The problem for most of us, whatever art form we are trying to find our feet in, is that we are usually inspired by people who are already very successful in our chosen field. It's therefore quite easy to feel that no matter how hard we try we are never going to reach the same standard. In one way it's true that we can't – years of experience and practice are something nobody can catch up with. However, the only thing that is stopping us from getting those years of experience under our own belts is being unwilling to put in the same hours and hard work our comedy heroes had to.

It's also true that no matter how much experience we gain and how hard we work we are never going to be able to write or perform exactly like the people we admire. But this is a good thing. As writers, we should always aim to be as unique as we can be, rather than just a pale imitation of somebody else.

On a more practical level, it is pointless beating ourselves up at the start because our original material isn't as good as the best of the stuff we see on television or in the cinema. Usually what we are comparing our own early work to is somebody else's *finished product*. That finished product came about through somebody taking their initial bits and pieces of ideas and scribblings, which probably weren't all that more polished or funny than our own, and then working on them and refining them. The strange thing about this way of thinking is that no matter how successful we become in our career, we still tend to make the same unfavourable comparisons. Some of the most experienced stand-up comedians will tell you that when waiting in the wings listening to the comic onstage before them, even if that person is the rankest beginner, they sound like the funniest comic in the world.

Out of curiosity I have asked professional musicians if they experience the same thing when listening to recordings on which their own work is featured. The answer has usually been yes. What sounds like wonderful music to us often sounds to the individual musician like a professional band of talented musicians in the midst of which is their own saxophone or piano honking or clinking away and sounding not quite as polished as the rest.

I hope that sharing the above thoughts will encourage you to take risks and try out new ideas without the pressure to be 'polished' at this stage. The polish will come later.

The good news about acknowledging that comedy writing doesn't need to start off polished is that it also doesn't need to be written in the same order that it will eventually be delivered in. We've already established that much humour stems from surprise and, in most jokes, that surprise element turns up in the punchline. So, given that jokes don't need to be written in the same order as in their finished versions, a very useful trick is to turn our attention from trying to create funny punchlines and instead address ourselves to writing the punchlines *first* and then coming up with the ideal straight lines to make them funny.

> Have you heard the joke about the doomsday cult?
>
> No? Oh well, it's not the end of the world.
>
> Have you heard the joke about the three eggs?
>
> Too bad.

Setting up jokes like this simply involves taking a well-known phrase such as 'It's not the end of the world' and then posing a question which, if that phrase is given as the answer, would make it funny, apt or ironic.

A variation of this technique which makes use of the 'embarrassment' trigger for humour is to take a cliché or phrase which is normally intended to be innocuous or even uplifting and think of the worst possible circumstances in which it might be used.

> A man runs into a doctor's surgery and says, 'I've got fifty-nine seconds to live.'
>
> 'Hang on,' says the doctor, 'I'll be with you in a minute.'

As already noted, finding humour in the kind of gaffes that usually make us cringe has worked very well for writers like Ricky Gervais and in TV shows like *Curb Your Enthusiasm*. It is also a technique that can be applied to topical humour. The following joke was written for morning radio just after reports of a fire in the Channel Tunnel:

> We know the engineers have been working 48-hour shifts to repair the damage, so we called them to offer our support. We can't understand why they were so ungrateful – I mean, all we said was 'Cheer up, guys – there's light at the end of the tunnel.'

This is a good example of 'pushing the boundaries' but only as far as will work for the particular job you are doing. What constitutes 'daring' on mainstream breakfast radio and what might be daring in a comedy club or late at night are of course very different things, and in the latter context this joke would be incredibly tame.

Radio stations have stricter rules, so we had obviously checked first that nobody had been injured in the fire, and of course we hadn't actually called the engineers – but the suggestion that somebody might have done so and then said something so inappropriate generated the required cringe/guilty laugh factor.

Since that news story happened a long time ago, for you to understand now what was funny about that joke on the day it was written and broadcast, I had to first fill in the context and recap the story it was based on.

This has always been the downside for comedians and writers who specialise in topical humour – jokes which are hilarious when the news story is fresh are often less funny or even incomprehensible once the story is forgotten or if the circumstances change. The problem is compounded for anyone writing topical comedy in our modern multi-media, 24/7 rolling-news-based world. Not only does the news change rapidly, but quite often there are only a very small number of news stories sufficiently big enough for you to be sure everyone in your audience is aware of them.

It's a far cry from the days when comedians could do topical humour based on storylines which were happening in the top TV shows of the time, and know that everyone would either have seen the show or at least have heard enough about the storyline to get the jokes based on it.

Today, we can all choose to watch our own favourite shows when and where we want, and filter out any news, TV or other information that doesn't appeal to us. The final episodes of shows like *Friends* and *M*A*S*H* were landmark television events watched by huge numbers of people around the world. The final episode of *Scrubs*, an equally good and long-running ensemble show made just a few years later, was also a landmark event – but only for people who were fans of *Scrubs*.

Some people are huge fans of *Star Trek* and know every episode of the original show off by heart, but even those of us who aren't dyed-in-the-wool 'trekkies' know enough about the show to spot when it is affectionately parodied by impressionists, stand-ups, and in contemporary comedy and sketch shows.

Later shows like *The Sopranos* or *Lost* are also cult favourites but fans of one may never have watched the other and there are plenty of people who, apart from having a vague awareness that one show is about a mafia family and the other is about airline passengers stranded somewhere, have never watched either show. A comedian doing material about them would either have to fill in lots of backstory before doing the related jokes or find that one half of the audience is loving the material while the other is just looking a little blank.

With this in mind, it is not surprising that comedians and writers often base much of their material on events, cultural references and characters from the past as much as on those in the news right now. Of course, as the reason for doing this is to create a sense of recognition and shared experience it has to be pitched right for the particular audience it is directed at.

As already mentioned, the core audience for stand-up comedy tends to be in the 18–35 age range. There will be enough parents – or at least people whose friends, brothers and sisters are now parents – at the 30-ish end of that audience to appreciate jokes about the trials of being a new parent, but if the audience in a particular venue is mainly composed of students from the other end of the age range, there is less likely to be a connection with that kind of material.

However, although not all of the 18–35-year-old core comedy audience will have been born in the 1970s or 1980s, reruns of shows from both eras are still very popular on current television schedules, and remakes and affectionate parodies of the hits of that era are still common in the movies or on stage. As a result, material about these years features quite frequently in contemporary comedy and seems to go down well with almost everyone. Go back any further and you usually have to work with the very broad strokes of what your audience might still be familiar with.

A plaque has recently been erected outside the house where Scarlett O' Hara actress Vivien Leigh grew up.

But they didn't fix it to the wall properly and next morning it was gone with the wind.

A few years ago, the same topical joke might have worked without having to mention Scarlett O'Hara to remind younger members of the audience what movie the actress was famous for.

A charity is auctioning a bedspread which used to belong to Mick Jagger. It dates back to the 1960s but it's still in perfect condition.

That's because a Rolling Stone gathers no moths.

An open-air Rolling Stones concert has been banned due to noise restrictions. The promoters have appealed to the city council.

But they couldn't get no satisfaction.

How does Keith Richards upload Facebook pictures?

From his Jumping Jack Flash Drive.

The Rolling Stones are an iconic enough band that even people who have never seen them perform are probably still aware enough of the name to 'get' the first joke above. The next two gags depend entirely on the audience being aware that two of the band's biggest hits were with the song titles contained in the punchlines. Interestingly, for many years Mick Jagger was probably the name most familiar to non-music fans as being in the Stones. For younger audiences today, thanks to the *Pirates of the Caribbean* movies, it may well be Keith Richards who is more likely to get name recognition.

You need to keep up to date with topical affairs if you intend to ply your trade in this area of comedy writing, but the key is not just knowing what is happening in the news, but more importantly *what is happening in the news that your audience is likely to have heard about or care about.* You will need to keep an eye on what people are talking about in terms of popular culture as well as what they no longer talk about or remember as well as they used to. Once a topic is past its 'sell by' date, it is time to drop the jokes on that subject from your repertoire no matter how well they once used to work and go and write some new ones.

Getting it together

What's the difference between a man and a beer bottle?

Nothing – they are both empty from the neck up.

We've already discussed combining two ideas to construct a joke, and just as there are very few sentences and phrases that won't yield some kind of double meaning if you probe them hard enough, there are very few objects in the world between which you can't find some connection if you put two of them together and examine them closely. The above joke obviously works on the basis that once you notice that a beer bottle is 'empty from the neck up' and you realise that 'empty from the neck up' is also a euphemism for 'stupid' you just need to find another object – in this case a man – that can be described in the same way for the purposes of humour.

You can apply a similar technique by linking two news stories together. For instance, on the same day the British newspapers were full of stories about bad behaviour on tour by the national football team, one of the smaller news features was a report on some research which had discovered that ladybirds weren't in fact the small innocent creatures portrayed in movies such as *A Bug's Life*.

Scientists have discovered that ladybirds are actually hungry, sex-crazed cannibals.

So they are being signed up to play for England.

77

Even if the story about the England team hadn't been in the papers on the same day, a glance at the research findings would have got most topical writers immediately looking for something to compare ladybirds to. This gag could easily have been adapted to suit a rock band, a group of politicians or misbehaving sports stars from some entirely different field. It's not hard to find somebody or some group of people misbehaving in the news any day of the week.

Exaggeration

Humour is sometimes a matter of perspective. As film director Mel Brooks reportedly observed: 'Comedy is when somebody falls down an open manhole. Tragedy is when I break my fingernail.'

Exaggeration and distortion have always been used by comedy writers as good, quick ways of taking simple ideas and turning them into usable jokes. For instance, take somebody who is a little bit lazy. Actually that's all of us at one time or another and it is not particularly funny. But let's exaggerate that idea a bit. Exactly how lazy was this person?

He was so lazy he thought manual labour was a Spanish politician'

He was so lazy even his flights of fancy were on auto pilot.

He was so lazy he had 'Mary' tattooed across his chest in honour of his wife.
(His wife's name was Catherine but Mary has fewer letters in it.)

He was so lazy he couldn't be bothered to do anything lazy to show how lazy he was.

The 'rule of three'

The rule of three is probably the best known of all joke formulas. Even if you have never heard it defined as a rule before, you'll almost certainly recognise the type of joke it describes.

An Irishman, an Englishman and a Chinese man are all travelling first class on a long-distance flight. Suddenly the Irishman looks out of the window. 'Look down there!' he says proudly. 'There goes Ireland!' Shortly afterwards the Englishman also looks down and he too gets excited. 'Look! There goes England.'

The Chinese man waits till the stewardess comes by with her trolley, grabs a pile of cups and plates and throws them out of the window. 'Look!' he shouts. 'There goes China!'

The Three Little Pigs, The Three Wise Men, The Three Musketeers – the number three seems to have a special significance in stories, in songs, in religion. Not being a mathematician or a philosopher I'm not exactly sure why this is, but I do know that its effectiveness in making jokes work relates to our old friend the element of surprise.

The human mind is very fond of patterns, so when something happens a certain number of times, our mind settles back and decides that a pattern has been created and that things are going to happen in the same pattern over and over again. It doesn't take many repetitions to set up that expectation of a pattern – in fact one repetition will do it. So in a typical 'rule of three' joke the first thing that happens is usually something reasonably believable (the Irishman spotting his country from the plane window), the second incident will be a very slight variation on the first one (the Englishman spotting England from the window), which sets up the expectation that the Chinese man will be the next to spot his country . . . or, as China is nowhere near Irish and English airspace, keep quiet. When he does something unexpected – grabbing the cups and plates (and reminding us that China is another word with more than one meaning) – the breaking of the pattern we were expecting makes us laugh.

How do we know the 'rule of three' works best? Well, if it was the 'rule of two' there wouldn't be enough repetitions to set up the pattern – here is the same joke without the Englishman.

An Irishman and a Chinese man are travelling first class on a long-distance flight. Suddenly the Irishman looks out of the window. 'Look down there!' he says proudly. 'There goes Ireland!'

The Chinese man waits till the stewardess comes by with her trolley, grabs a pile of cups and plates and throws them out of the window. 'Look!' he shouts. 'There goes China!'

The punchline is still there, but as you can see it feels a lot weaker as there haven't been enough repetitions to set up the pattern. However, increasing the number of repetitions above three doesn't make the joke any funnier – in fact it slows the pace up and makes it difficult to maintain our interest long enough to enjoy the punchline. Here's the joke again with an extra cast member:

An Irishman, an Englishman, a Frenchman and a Chinese man are all travelling first class on a long-distance flight. Suddenly the Irishman looks out of the window. 'Look down there!' he says proudly. 'There goes Ireland!' Shortly afterwards the Englishman also looks down and he too gets excited. 'Look! There goes England.'

A little later the Frenchman looks out of the window and shouts, 'Look, there goes France!'

The Chinese man waits till the stewardess comes by with her trolley, grabs a pile of cups and plates . . . and then puts them back again as he realises the joke has gone on too long and the audience has fallen asleep.

Stereotypes

'Brevity is the soul of wit,' said Shakespeare, and this is certainly true for the comedy writer who wants to fit as many laughs as possible into the short time usually available for a broadcast routine. For this reason stereotypes are often used as a means of giving the hearer the maximum amount of information needed to understand a joke in the minimum amount of time.

In Chapter One we discussed the often derogatory racial stereotypes that have always been a part of certain types of comedy – most 'Irishman, Englishman and Chinese man'-type jokes would be closer in theme to this kind of humour than the more playful one we used for our 'rule of three' example above. But even if that kind of stereotyping isn't something you would consider, it can be hard to produce a steady stream of gags without occasionally relying on stock characters and particular traits associated with various professions. In the comedy world bankers and lawyers are usually money-orientated if not downright crooked while female teachers and librarians tend to be mousy and repressed (at least until they take their glasses off and shake out their hair, whereupon they invariably transform into pouting temptresses).

Perception is often as significant as truth – for example, no matter how many improvements are made to the British National Health Service, jokes about the NHS tend to be based on the assumption that accessing any of its services will take a very long time.

Viagra is to be made available from the NHS.

You're guaranteed an erection but you'll have to wait two years.

Just like the effects of Viagra, popular stereotypes of how the rich and famous live can last for a long time too. The joke below was written when pop singer Madonna was pregnant:

Doctors say they have seen a scan and Madonna's baby looks very healthy.

And so do the twelve bodyguards surrounding it.

Of course, since having her own child, Madonna has also been in the news for adopting children, as have several other 'A-listers' such as Angelina Jolie.

As advocated by Sacha Baron Cohen's spoiled male model character in spoof documentary *Bruno* the practice of 'adopting children from third-world countries' has now joined 'constantly being surrounded by bodyguards' in the comedy writers' list of stereotypical celebrity behaviours.

Reusable gags

It is not hard to see how the joke about Madonna quoted above could be updated and recycled whenever any other female celebrity with a reputation for travelling with an entourage is expecting. And who could blame a writer with a quota of topical jokes to meet and a deadline close at hand if they did just that?

Comedians often complain that singers have life very easy. When Frank Sinatra sang 'My Way' for the thousandth time or when Beyoncé sings 'All the Single Ladies', no shouts of 'Get off, heard it before!' rend the air. For a comedian or comedy writer without that 'repeat' option it is very important to keep coming up with fresh new material not just from a commercial point of view but also because like any other muscle, comedy writing skills need to be kept in good condition whether you are working or not.

Recycling and updating material you have previously used is good business sense and the art of knowing when and how to update it so that it still sounds like new material is a challenge that in itself helps polish the writer's skills. One of the things which makes this recycling possible is the tendency of history and human behaviour to repeat themselves with reassuring regularity.

During a recent election a married politician was in all the tabloid papers over an alleged affair with a much younger woman and lines like the one below were rife:

The election is in full swing, so all the politicians are out kissing babies.

Or, in (Name of politician's) case, dating them.

82

Because 'kissing babies at election time' is seen as 'stock politician behaviour' as much as having bodyguards is stock behaviour for celebrities, and because it is almost inevitable that other politicians in this country and other countries will be caught in similar compromising positions with younger ladies, simply slot the appropriate legislator's name into the space provided next time this type of story pops up and the joke will seem fresh and new all over again.

Other topical jokes have been recycled not just from era to era but from one topic to another. One of the best remembered sketches from the British satirical series *Spitting Image* – which used puppet effigies of the great and good to often savage effect – was a scene in which then Prime Minister Margaret Thatcher is in a restaurant with a group of her cabinet ministers. Mrs T orders a meat dish.

'What about the vegetables?' asks the waiter.

'They'll have the same as me.'

Years later, the 'vegetable' joke still crops up regularly, not just about the leader of whatever political party is not doing so well in the polls but also with the lead character switched to being the manager or coach of any well-known sports team which has lost a couple of games in a row.

Children's jokes are, as we have already seen, very good examples of basic joke-writing mechanisms at work in their rawest form, but are usually a bit too obvious to use regularly in commercial comedy writing. However, there are occasions when their basic joke structures can be recycled in a way which does produce usable topical humour.

You are probably familiar with the kind of joke which goes:

Have you heard the joke about the bed?

It hasn't been made up yet.

Have you heard the one about the broken pencil?

There's not much point to it.

On live radio we found it useful to adapt this kind of joke to cover the inevitable delays and non-appearances of guests who got caught in early-morning traffic or pulled out for other last-minute reasons:

> We were expecting celebrity stylist Vidal Sassoon to join us for this part of the show, but he's been delayed.
>
> He must be having a bad hair day.

> At the top of the show we promised you an exclusive interview with a celebrity chef. But we've now been told he can't make it.
>
> Seems like he's got too much on his plate.

As this kind of line seemed to be very popular, we eventually got to the point of inventing non-existent guests so that we could get jokes out of their inevitable non-appearance:

> This morning we were going to do a phone interview with an escapologist.
>
> But apparently he's tied up at the moment.

> We invited the 'Preacher of the Year' to come on the show and give us some highlights of his prize-winning sermon on 'Humility'.
>
> But he says he's too famous now to bother with the likes of us.

Just tell the truth

Telling a friend they look fine while secretly thinking their dress looks dreadful. Saying we're really enjoying a boring party when we'd actually rather be undergoing dental surgery (without anaesthetic). Assuring loved ones that another pair of socks is exactly what we wanted for Christmas no matter how horrible they are. Most of us spend so much time saying what we think we ought to say rather than what we actually mean, that sometimes the fastest way to generate surprise and laughter is simply to tell the truth.

For centuries it has been the special role of the jester to say things out loud that most of us may well be thinking but which we would be afraid to express in words. Some jesters were even allowed the ultimate privilege of being the only person who could poke fun at the appearance and personal quirks of the king himself and get away with it. (Of course if the king was having a bad day, the jester ran the risk of discovering that 'dying on stage' wasn't just a comedy euphemism.)

The modern comedy writer can also cut through layers of hypocrisy and 'spin' simply by stating the truth.

> The World Food Summit. That's where all the world leaders get together to discuss solutions to global poverty and starvation.
>
> And then go for a really expensive meal.

Although much humour relies on twist endings, double meanings and taking everyday situations in illogical directions, applying extreme logic and taking a train of thought to its ultimate end result can also generate laughter:

> The town council has had expensive surveillance systems installed in every street to deter burglaries.
>
> Makes sense – why bother breaking into a house when you can steal state-of-the-art camera equipment straight off the wall?

Applying this to our tattoo theme might produce the following:

> I was thinking about getting a tattoo, but I was worried about the pain. My friend suggested that if I drank some whisky beforehand I wouldn't feel a thing.
>
> He was right – after a few bottles I was too drunk to turn up for the appointment.

Visual comedy

Although it is undeniable that much comedy relies on words, when it works well visual comedy is not just surprising and fun but has obvious advantages in translating better to a wider range of international markets.

In some ways every sort of comedy should be visual even when it is on the radio or in a stand-up routine because the most effective words are the ones which create pictures. As with other kinds of comedy, there are many 'standard' visual jokes which can be adapted depending on the topic you are working on. For instance, the subject of tattoos might allow us to adapt a very old sight gag which more usually concerns an artist working on a picture. In our version we see the tattoo artist working on a customer. As the customer has his back to us, and the tattoo artist is working behind him, we don't see what he is drawing, just that he is using his thumb to measure distances and angles in the way artists often do. After much gesturing the tattoo is finally revealed as being a big picture of the artist's thumb. Just as in a written joke where we usually reveal the punchline at the very end, visual jokes often depend on revealing their punchline at the last minute. We'll discuss this in more detail when we look at 'quickie' sketches in Chapter Five.

Confirmations and contradictions

If you have read this far into the chapter, you may well have felt that some of the pieces of advice given so far have been mutually exclusive. For instance, I've just finished telling you that truth is a very important element in comedy when just a few pages ago our theme was that exaggeration is a key feature in making jokes work. Essentially, our aim is give you a whole range of different suggestions you can use in your own comic writing. Some of these ideas will work very well with one particular topic or theme, while other news items or points of view may lend themselves to a different approach. But it really shouldn't be a surprise that our range of joke-writing techniques throws up some contradictions because life itself is riddled with contradictions. Recognising that fact can be a very good indicator of where the comedy may be found in something you are writing about.

Some of my favourite comedy is drawn from the difference between what we think we are and what we actually are, not to mention what we say and what we do. Oliver Hardy, Bud Abbott, Ernie Wise and the other great double-act 'straight' men were always very aware that the reason their characters were more ridiculous than their more overtly comic counterparts like Stan Laurel, Lou Costello or Eric Morecambe was because they thought they were *less* ridiculous than the other member of the double act. It was actually this pomposity which made them funny in their own way. In both the UK and US versions of *The Office*, lead characters David Brent and Michael Scott completely believe that they are excellent people managers – yet everything they say and do confirms exactly the opposite.

One very simple joke technique based on contradictions like these is to come up with a statement of fact, and then tag on a line or action that reflects the complete opposite.

The Archbishop of Canterbury says horoscopes are just super-stitious rubbish.

But then he's bound to be sceptical – he's a Taurus.

A twist on this technique is to use an ending that appears to contradict the beginning but in fact confirms it.

Women's groups have accused the government of being sexist and patronising.

The government has promised to take this on board, and told them not to worry their pretty little heads about it any further.

We've looked at lots of different types of joke in this chapter, and, as we have already noted, while there may not be thousands of basic joke structures, there are undoubtably thousands of variations on those basic jokes.

While all of the joke types I have discussed so far are ones which I have personally found helpful over many years of working to tight deadlines, there may well be favourites of yours that we haven't looked at in detail. If there is a particular gag you have come across which made you think 'I wish I had written that one', the best way to approach it is not to copy it outright, but to really analyse it in terms of structure and see if you can apply the same structure to the ideas that come out of your own brainstorming. If you're new to this process, it may seem like a lot of work to do at first, but like any new skill, with a bit of regular practice you will be surprised how quickly your brain can learn to focus on a topic, brainstorm lots of related ideas, and then filter out the most promising ones. You can then run them through your mental memory bank of effective joke structures to turn those ideas into twenty, forty or even seventy jokes. The 'quota' aspect of this process is very important. As noted before, I didn't say we were aiming for twenty, forty or seventy *good* jokes. Once you have your jokes in the right quantity, then you can start thinking in terms of quality and decide which ones are never going to work and which ones can be sent out to face the audience on the air, in the comedy club or in script form.

Remember that even jokes which don't quite work at the moment may work for a slightly different subject or with a bit more thought at some other time – smart writers keep a file of all their ideas and thoughts for future reference and having a quick look through that file is often part of their regular comedy-writing routine.

To help motivate you through the hours of practice it can require to get your comedy-writing brain up to speed and keep it there, it might just be worth reminding yourself of the reason why so many professional comedy writers put themselves through such a labour-intensive production process with such regularity. Yes, it's sometimes the satisfaction of getting paid for your work, but for most of us a far greater satisfaction comes from sitting in a studio or theatre audience, watching TV with friends and family at home or peeking out from backstage during a show, to see and hear people laughing out loud at a line we have written. It's equally exciting to see something we created get re-tweeted or emailed around the world often just a few hours after it was originally just a germ of an idea on our brainstorm list.

Of course, for this to happen all the jokes we have manufactured have to find their way into organised routines, scripts or speeches. This is what we will start to look at in our next chapter.

Over to you . . .

1 Time to build up your own joke-writing muscles – and like any other kind of muscle building, repetition is the key. Pick a set time each day for a week – whether morning, midday or evening is up to you, but it helps to pick a time when you are freshest. Choose ten news stories, large or small, from each day's news and come up with as many jokes on each topic as you can using the brainstorming method described in this chapter.

2 After each session, pick the ten jokes you think work best and from them decide which you think are your top five. Then try all ten jokes on family and friends (or at least the people in each category who will give you an honest opinion). Do your top five match theirs? Which types of joke consistently get the best response for you? Knowing your strengths as a writer is very important and often something your audience may have a different perspective on.

3 As you continue to practise your joke writing, try to keep abreast of as much topical comedy as you can – whether it's daily and weekly satirical TV shows, comedy-orientated blogs and newspaper columns, topical cartoons, or going to see live comics who regularly cover the news. Pay particular attention to jokes on the same news stories you have used. You can learn a lot from how your 'competition' approaches the same material, both in terms of what they did that worked better and what you have come up with that they may not have thought of.

4

Writing Comedy Routines

A friend of mine once suggested that because stand-up comedy is such a hard thing to be a beginner at, aspiring stand-ups should be like singers doing 'cover versions'. The idea was that they should spend the first few months of their careers telling other people's jokes until they got used to the actual business of performing on stage, at which point they could then deliver their own original material effectively.

I can't quite agree with this strategy – I think both writers and comedians need to be working at developing a reputation for originality from the beginning of their careers – but I do understand the thinking behind it. Performing and writing are two separate and equally challenging skills and not everyone has the talent or the dedication to learn to juggle both effectively.

In noting this, I am very aware that some people reading these pages may well be performers in their own right. Indeed some of the most encouraging responses to previous editions of this book have come from working stand-ups, presenters and broadcasters who have found it useful in honing their own material.

For comedy writers who do not perform, the days when comics could afford to employ personal writers are, as noted earlier, long gone. In terms of getting paid to write for comedians you are now more likely to be hired to do so by a third party, usually a TV production company, and you will probably be writing for more than one performer. 'Stand-up style' one-liners and topical humour have also become a much bigger factor in many other styles of speeches and presentations in addition to traditional stand-up, and it is often in these fields that the modern comedy writer sells their skills.

With this in mind we are going to take a broader view of writing a comedy routine than just stand-up, and set out an approach which will work well whether the person you are writing for is yourself or somebody else, and whether your end product is a traditional stand-up routine or some other form of presentation such as a business, political or motivational speech which relies principally on one person standing up and speaking in public.

As this is a comedy writing book, it makes sense to work through the creation of an overtly comic routine as our main example, but it shouldn't be too difficult for you (or the person you are writing for) to judge how much or how little comedy you include in other kinds of speeches or presentations. Certainly, if you can learn to write a comedy routine which gets laughs all the way through, you shouldn't have too much of a problem getting the right laughs in the right places in other scripting projects.

Similarly, to ensure that the principles here work for the maximum number of people, we will concentrate on creating routines from the point of view of a writer producing material for *somebody else* to perform, although as we will see later, the same methods should work just as well if you are writing for yourself.

First, catch your comic

The first step in writing any comedy routine is being clear on who we are going to write it for. For the purposes of developing your skills in this area, it is certainly worth selecting a few of your own favourite performers or speakers as 'guinea pigs' to tailor your sample material to. If possible, choose performers or speakers who are making a name for themselves in today's market. There is little point in becoming the ideal writer for star names who have retired or passed away (although you can still learn a huge amount by studying and applying the techniques they and their writers used to make them stars in their own era). You may or may not feel that is worth actually pitching your finished material to your chosen 'client', although the chances are that if they are already established they already work with whatever writers they are used to. Nevertheless, before we knuckle down to writing it is still worth beginning by looking at how to make contact with a potential client, as the etiquette involved is the best way to introduce yourself to anyone you intend to work with.

Even in the days when big-name comics, public speakers and presenters were more likely to directly employ writers, bringing your work to their attention rarely happened via contact with the stars themselves. Today, famous names (and their producers and directors) may appear to be much more accessible via websites, email or on Twitter, but this is usually a public relations illusion. When it comes to doing business, your initial contact with an established comedian, presenter or public speaker is almost always going to be via a third party, whether that is a press officer, a personal assistant or their agent.

In fact at the higher levels of the US comedy scene, even trying to make contact via their agent may not get you very far. You will usually be expected to have your own agent to do the contacting if you want to be taken seriously!

We'll discuss agents and how they relate to writers in more detail in Chapter Six. For now, if the person you are seeking to write for regularly appears on television you can contact the production company or network for which they last worked and from there you should be able to get some agent contact details. These details may also be listed under the 'bookings' section of their website, in the small print of tour brochures or in the credits of any spin-off books or DVD material.

Bear in mind that since the days of silent movies, almost everyone in the public eye receives huge swathes of fan mail, junk mail and sometimes completely random and disturbing mail often just because they are in the public eye. The internet has only served to increase this phenomenon to avalanche proportions. The clearer and more businesslike you can make your proposal the more chance there is of it being identified as something actually worth reading.

Send a short, polite letter or email care of the performer's agent or other official contact, telling them why you like their work, and more importantly why you think your writing would be good for them. (You'll note that 'good for *them*' is the important factor here. How much it might help your own career is not relevant to anyone except you.) Make it clear that the sample material you have enclosed or attached is your own original work, that it hasn't been used by anyone else, and that if they like it but feel it's not quite right you'll be happy to try again based on clearer instructions.

Don't send a huge wad of gags or routines – a couple of pages of your best work should be enough to whet their appetites. We'll look at the practicalities of submitting work, whether electronically or physically, in Chapter Six, but however you make your approach, allow a reasonable amount of time to pass before you call or email to chase up a response. After all, one of the reasons agents and managers are employed in the first place is to stop people hassling their clients.

If your writing is strong enough, if you have tailored your material sufficiently well to your prospective client's personality and style and maybe if you're just a little bit lucky, you should hear back eventually.

Even if the end result isn't an actual sale, you may at least get some valuable comments and feedback on your work. If the response is in any way positive you may want to keep sending in material at regular intervals – but always allowing a reasonable amount of time between them and, of course, making sure any previous feedback has been incorporated into the new stuff. A consistent source of good quality material is always going to be more attractive to a client than somebody who comes up with a good joke or routine once in a blue moon.

Continuing to demonstrate commitment, perseverance and ongoing interest (as long as these qualities are communicated in a professional rather than obsessive way) may just be enough to overcome any initial reluctance to use your material. How much effort you are prepared to put into the 'wooing' process depends on how much you want to work with this particular comedian, speaker or performer, but whatever the eventual outcome, the practice you get is bound to improve your skills both in terms of tailoring your work to a client's needs and also in the ongoing process of marketing your work in a determined but professional manner.

93

As we have already noted, the one major factor which can make it difficult to get work from bigger-name comedians and performers is that they may already have established a relationship with a regular writer or group of writers at an earlier stage of their careers. While such loyalty is admirable it may not allow room for any new writers – not even one as talented as you.

With this in mind, you may also want to take yourself down to your local comedy club or theatre to see if there are any up-and-coming acts you might like to write for. Although the chances of either getting paid or becoming well known from working at this level are almost non-existent, if you approach your mission correctly you have a much better chance of actually hearing your material performed in front of an audience. Because job satisfaction is likely to be the only reward for this kind of comedy writing, it makes sense for you to look for performers who have qualities you genuinely like as opposed to performers you think might become famous in a couple of years. The ideal scenario is obviously to find a combination of both. Whether or not you are getting paid, if you do decide to connect your up-and-coming writing skills to some up-and-coming performing talent, it is only worthwhile if both of you approach the task as diligently and with the same focus as you would if they were already a big-name comedian and you were a highly paid professional writer.

After all, one of the key aims of this exercise is to develop a body of professional quality work that you'll be able to refer to, and prove your credentials with, as you start to build your own career in the professional writing world.

Once you've discovered your potential rising star, it's time to study them in detail, just as you would any client you write for. Ask yourself if their main strength is on the performance side or if they already have strong material. If the performance area is where they shine, do you think you could write material that would play better to the person's strengths and stage persona than the lines they are currently using? If they already have strong material, what areas do you feel you could build on to complement the performer's own particular writing skills?

Try to see them perform in a number of different venues and circumstances so that you get a good general overview of their current work. It's probably best to introduce yourself as a writer sooner rather than later unless you want to get accused of being a stalker, and especially important to bear in mind if you are a male writer wanting to work with a female performer or speaker. Even at the very lower end of the entertainment and media worlds, anyone who steps into the spotlight is almost guaranteed to get approached on a regular basis by all manner of people offering strange, useless and unsolicited 'advice', not to mention offers of management, stupid, obscene and unfunny jokes and many other forms of unwanted personal harassment. As a result, don't be too surprised if even your politest initial approach after a show is received very warily. How you get over this wariness is down to your own people skills (often just as important to your success as a writer as the quality of your work).

Most people should respond well to somebody showing genuine interest and knowledge of their work – particularly if you start off by telling them what you genuinely *like* about it before launching into a long list of the things you'd change. If you have already written some material you think might be suitable, most performers should be flattered enough to take a look, or at the very least too curious not to.

It is, of course, entirely up to you whether you decide to introduce yourself in person to the performer you have been studying or send them an email via their website. If you decide that your first approach will be made online, the advice already given about being polite, professional and clear about your intentions is equally relevant.

It goes without saying that if you are giving your sample material to a performer face to face, neatly typed and printed pages in a clean envelope or a fresh disk clearly labelled are liable to be taken a lot more seriously than something crumpled and grubby thrust into their hands in the back of a comedy club.

However you deliver your stuff, if they like it, they may try one or two lines out at their next gig or booking and if that works . . . well, I'm tempted to write that you'll both live happily ever after but that's not always the case. What will probably happen is that the performer may be interested in using your work, but as a relative beginner it's very unlikely that they will have the financial resources to offer more than a token payment if they can afford payment at all. We'll be looking at contracts more closely in our chapter on a comedy writing career, but the bottom line is that whenever you are planning to work with somebody, whether formally or informally, it is always a good idea to make sure both parties are clear on what the deal involves, not only in relation to finances but concerning writing credits too.

Credit is an important issue in all aspects of writing – after all, it is the means by which an aspiring writer establishes their reputation – but it is a particularly important and often sensitive issue when it comes to comedy writing,

In broadcast and theatrical comedy, the writers' credits are, as a matter of course, included along with the director, the producer, the make-up people and everyone else who has contributed to the production. However, when it comes to writing for an individual comedian or for a speaker with a reputation for humour, there are differing schools of thought.

Many comics who are also good writers get understandably annoyed at comments along the lines of 'loved your act, who writes your material?', as if to suggest they couldn't possibly have come up with something funny on their own. (Sadly this particularly happens to female comedians because for some reason, despite the huge number of talented women who are currently working in comedy, not to mention comedy legends like Fanny Brice, Phyllis Diller, Joan Rivers and Whoopi Goldberg, who forged the way in previous eras, there is still a perception that women somehow can't be funny without the help of a man.) It's certainly true that part of the 'magic' of a good comedy routine is the illusion that the performer is coming up with fresh witty things to say on the spot rather than repeating lines that have been written, pre-prepared or rehearsed. For all these reasons, some comics may be wary of openly admitting to working with a writer. Other comics realise that to be able to tell people they now work with a writer or co-writer is actually an indication that their act is progressing in a field where any sense of status or progression can often be very hard to acquire.

When you do connect with a comic or performer and find that you can work well together, the 'honeymoon period' can be very exciting. That's all the more reason for the two of you to agree right from the start on what happens if this success starts to translate into real money and more high-profile work, as it is often at this point that tensions creep in.

There are, of course, many cases of performers who have been tremendously loyal to the comedy partners who have helped them reach star status. American comedy legend Jimmy Durante was a huge star for well over half a century, but throughout his career would always find work in his show for Eddie Jackson and Lou Clayton, his original 1920s writing and performing partners. But there are also well-known stories of less happy endings – perhaps the most famous UK example was one of the country's first radio and TV superstars, Tony Hancock, who dropped his writing team Galton and Simpson along with the supporting cast who had all been key factors in his success. Most critics trace the collapse of Hancock's career and resulting slide into depression and eventual suicide to this insecurity-driven mistake.

While not every rise to fame will be as spectacular as Durante's or fall from grace as tragic as Hancock's, the difficulty with formalising an agreement at the early stage of any working relationship, especially an experimental one, is that it can be a bit like trying to write a prenuptial agreement after just a couple of dates. This is especially true when dealing with comedians who, by their nature, can often be solitary and insecure individuals. Too much formality and commitment at the beginning of the relationship can scare them away. However, being clear about what you want and expect from the relationship is an important part of being professional.

Given that both of you are individuals developing your respective careers, it is not unlikely that your career goals will in any case be different. In addition to the basics, such as how any money that results from working together is divided and whether or not you get credited in public as the writer, there are other issues such as how much time you are prepared to invest in working together and whether you are going to work only for this one comedian or speaker or for other people too, which also need to be clear from the beginning.

In the latter case, my personal opinion is that no matter how closely or amicably you work with a particular performer, it is no bad thing to work with other performers and even other co-writers too. It's unlikely, given the basic insecurity of the entertainment business and the comedy business in particular, that every comic you work with will *like* this arrangement. There's undeniably something about the loneliness of the job which makes individual comedians very competitive towards each other. But if they truly value your work and your personal integrity – in other words, that you are not creating similar jokes for other comics – they will learn to accept the situation.

In any case, the whole skill of the professional writer is to come up with material which is especially tailored to the individual comic or speaker so duplication problems shouldn't arise.

A close relationship with a performer which maintains some professional detachment is also of advantage to the performer themselves. As public speaking and stand-up, even in this multi-media age, are still essentially one-person occupations, it is very difficult for a comic or speaker to get a truly objective impression of how their act or persona comes across from the audience's point of view. Even video or audio recordings of the act, while helpful for later reflection, can't quite capture the intimacy and immediacy of watching the performance 'in the moment'.

Working with a good writer gives the performer the chance to have somebody with an expert eye who is 'on their side' out front, giving them an outside perspective on how the act is going over, from rehearsal to performance stage. Then you can both start working together to correct what doesn't work and build on what does work until it works even better.

Getting into the routines

Despite my cautioning you about the need to establish sensible agreements from the start when working with other performers and writers, I should point out that I have had very good relations with most of the people I have personally collaborated with and I am sure this will be the case for you too.

As your ongoing relationship with a particular performer develops, the process of 'writing for them' or 'writing together' may get less formal. In my own case the 'writing' process with regular clients or writing partners often involves us getting together in a room, brainstorming and chatting through all the possibilities thrown up by a story or topic they want to cover, and often even acting out bits of comedy there and then. Then I take away my notes and polish the results into a rough script for further mutual discussion, as does the other party if they are a writer too.

However, in order to look at the practicalities of writing the kind of quality speeches, presentations and comedy routines which will help you develop productive ongoing relationships, let's assume that at this point your relationship with the person who will be performing your work is more formal and that you will be working alone on material which you will be submitting on a page or via email, without too much preliminary discussion. In other words, our aim is a complete routine that already works even before the client adds their own input.

In Chapter 3, we used a step-by-step process of brainstorming and then refining our ideas to generate jokes (hopefully you have been practising regularly since then) and we will be using a similar method to develop our comedy routines and speeches.

Of course, just as there are very basic jokes which almost anyone can make up, there is also a very basic way of 'writing a routine' which is still widely used and not just by amateurs. This involves writing (or, more usually, stealing from other sources) a random collection of jokes and stringing them together in no particular order to fill the allotted time.

I'm not suggesting that this approach never works. It very much depends on the strength of the individual jokes and even more on how engaging and funny the stage persona of the performer delivering the material is. But, from the professional writer's point of view, we will be aiming to produce something more structured.

As with the stunt arranger we previously referred to, often the best indication that the writer has done their work well is that this underlying structure won't be overtly visible, but it is this behind-the-scenes work which underpins most successful comic performances and which can turn even a seemingly random collection of jokes, trains of thought and observations into a viable and satisfying whole.

Let's now pick a topic for our sample routine and start brainstorming jokes . . . or rather, let's not. Because, from the professional point of view, there are three very important questions we need to ask first:

1 What kind of routine is needed and how much time is available for it?
2 What audience is this routine aimed at?
3 What is my point of view in this routine? (For many comedy writers and fans, this is the most important question of all.)

Let's take them in the order they are set out above.

What kind of routine is needed and how much time is available?

For comedy writers in particular, building a successful career involves having a very good understanding of time.

As I am sure is becoming clear, building a career is certainly going to take time. It also helps a lot in terms of getting hired – and, even more importantly, getting re-hired – if we learn to deliver good quality material within the time allowed by whatever deadline has been given to us.

But as most comedy writing is designed to be performed or broadcast in particular time slots, one of the key skills a writer also needs is to have a good understanding of the relationship between the words we type on a page or on a screen and the time it will actually take to read or perform those words out loud.

This requirement is probably most relevant when it comes to writing material for broadcast – it would obviously be a bad idea for a live routine or speech to carry on past the end time of a live broadcast and delay either the start of the news programme following it or, perhaps even more disastrously for the producers, the commercials which have paid for the show in the first place. Of course, if this did look like happening on a live show it is much more likely that the routine would simply be cut off in mid-flow. In a recorded programme, the offending routine would simply be edited down to the correct length regardless of whether the jokes still made sense or not. Less common now, but a more frequent occurrence during the early days of live broadcasting, was the equally big error of 'under-running' when there wasn't enough pre-prepared material to fill the required broadcast slot.

It was often incidents like this which made stars out of comics like the USA's Steve Allen or the UK's Bob Monkhouse, both of whom were adept at coming up with ad-libbed material to fill unexpected delays and gaps.

Whether the problem is too many words or too few, not being able to provide material which runs to the required time reflects very badly on the writer.

When a performance is live, it may seem that there isn't quite as much necessity to work strictly to time. However, while an audience may be only too happy if a popular comic does more encores than originally scheduled, comedy club bookers, festival production managers and corporate event organisers are much less likely to be amused.

So much for the negative consequences of not learning to write to time. For a more positive motivation, you may remember those highly paid writers we mentioned in Chapter Two who provide links for non comedy-based TV shows or for the bigger budget TV and radio commercials. In many cases their value to the producers who pay their salaries comes not just because they can write good quality comedy, but because they can write good quality comedy to fit very short timescales – in many cases as short as thirty seconds for a commercial. And it's not unusual for the copywriter and voice-over artist to be asked to adjust that thirty-second script in very precise increments – perhaps to twenty-eight seconds or maybe to twenty-six seconds – as the commercial comes together. It's a real art form, and the only way to get a feel for how much writing you need to fill a designated time slot is to get into the habit of reading your work out loud and timing it, allowing for pauses and leaving space for laughs. You'll also need to learn how to adjust your own sense of timing to match the timing of the different speakers and comedians you may write for.

For now, let's take a quick overview of some of the more typical time slots you may be asked to fill. Although we are focusing on typical time frames for stand-up comedy routines (and even these 'standard' times are not hard-and-fast rules), they coincide very well with the attention span of the average audience and therefore are also well worth bearing in mind when producing speeches, presentations and other kinds of writing.

'Open' or 'try-out' spots

As the name suggests, these very short routines (which can some-times be as short as two minutes and are usually not much longer than five) have long been the accepted route by which newer comedians can dip their toes in the waters of live performing. Usually 'open mike' spots are performed for no payment in the hope that if they go well, the comic will then be offered a paid gig at the same club. Since the comedy circuit has become more slick and commercial, this type of rough-and-ready open spot is less universal than it once was, and is now usually confined to smaller clubs or amateur comedy nights in the upstairs rooms of bars or colleges. The larger agencies and comedy venues do still try out new acts but often in the more formal 'talent show' format. After all, if you have to audition people, why not pick a format that allows you to sell tickets at the same time? Whether it is for an ordinary open mike spot or a big talent show, five minutes may not seem like a very challenging time span to have to write for or perform but that's only if you have never had the experience of spending even a minute or two on stage with jokes which have fallen flat.

However, when your writing skills are firing on all cylinders, five minutes can seem a frustratingly short period in which to make a real impact.

Nevertheless, being able to make the best of this very short type of spot is crucial for the comedy writer and not only at the entry-level stage. Even when a comedy career progresses and the comic is doing much longer live shows, the first 'break' into broadcasting, with all the increased profile and larger income that can result, will probably be via a very short slot on a talk show or on a talent show. A really good short routine should take a long time to develop and should be consistently polished and tightened until it is as near perfect as it can be. And once that five-minute spot is working the next step up is usually . . .

Ten-minute spots

Also called 'half spots', comedy routines which fit into this rough time frame are usually the first paid work a comedian gets – they also offer scope to establish the comedian's persona more strongly, and perhaps add a little more variety to the routine in terms of topics and ideas. It's usually when performers start doing ten-minute spots that it becomes easier to work out who is primarily a good comedy performer (not that there is anything wrong with just being that) and which performers also have writing skills. In the former case, if you are a regular comedy club goer you many well begin to recognise 'ten-minute spots' which are in actual fact the comedian's original five-minute spot stretched out to twice the length with very weak extra material. If it's a comic you would like to write for, and you are familiar with their original act, you might want to think about what you can offer them in terms of expanding their act in a stronger way, and perhaps even suggest that to them – always taking care to present your suggestions in a positive way, of course.

Perhaps the popularity of the ten-minute time slot stems from the advice given by many preachers, teachers and public speakers down through the ages to keep speeches to around eight minutes, as beyond this point, it is widely believed, audience minds start to wander. Certainly it is part of the writer's job to ensure this wandering doesn't happen – whether a spot is five or ten minutes long. A good attention (and laughter) grabbing opening is obviously important as is a strong ending, but in this longer spot it is the quality of what comes between those two points that should eventually allow the comic to graduate to the working performer's 'bread and butter' routine . . .

The full set

For comics, singers or any other kind of performer a good twenty minutes or so of material allows a great deal of scope for finding regular work. It can be fitted neatly into a variety show at whatever point in the schedule the performer's reputation and expertise merits (the more successful the comic the more likely they are to be the headliner or bill topper who comes on at the end). It can also be programmed in as a key feature of a corporate event. At many corporate or dinner-and-dancing-type events, twenty minutes may be all that is required of the performer and, for very well-known or in-demand performers, the payment for those twenty minutes can be very substantial indeed.

We have already identified broadcast as one of the more lucrative markets for comedy, but there are plenty of performers and speakers who either deliberately, or simply because they are not the TV 'flavour of the month', do the vast majority of their performing away from the cameras. The downside in terms of lack of screen fame can often be compensated for by the ability to use what is basically the same twenty-minute act in different venues for years and even decades without having to come up with anything new.

Of course, as with the other time slots we have covered, this type of spot can vary greatly in actual length – a headline act may well perform an 'extended set' lasting anything from forty minutes to an hour. Even when twenty minutes actually *does* mean twenty minutes, there is a lot of scope for writer and comedian to offer audiences a well-structured and complete experience, with a beginning, middle and end and even room to introduce entertaining digressions with different characters, musical comedy or other special features along the way.

One-person show

At comedy and theatre festivals all over the world, comedians can present their one-person shows to audiences of comedy fans, festival-goers and, most importantly, comedy producers and TV scouts looking for the next big thing. The one-person show typically lasts around an hour as this timing works very well with festival schedules. Sometimes the show is a natural expansion of an existing routine and sometimes it is a specially written show (which may still include much of the comic's regular set but adapted to fit the main theme). In the latter case, a writer or director's input can be very useful.

Many first shows are biographical, often dealing with the comedian's own life story or something they are passionate about. Fondly remembered TV shows, movies or literary series are popular themes, whether mocked mercilessly or affection-ately, although subjects as diverse as ukulele playing, pottery and engineering have all had successful shows based on them. Another popular approach is to come up with a crazy challenge such as 'crossing every road in the country dressed as a chicken' and then construct a show by detailing what happened when you carried the challenge out, complete with slides, videos and other illustrations. (If the comedian tells the story particularly well, this technique has also been known to result in book deals or even a TV series.) For comedians who base their set on charac-ter comedy, the one-person show often requires a rudimentary plot so that they can introduce each character at the appropriate points. (Some good ideas from the writer may also be needed for what can be happening on stage to keep the audience amused while the comic is doing costume changes.)

Who is the audience?

This is the second important question we need to ask before starting work on our routine and one which may have several answers. Obviously the general age make-up of the audience will have a bearing on the kind of material you put in the routine. If you are thinking that a good performer and a good writer should be able to make any material work for any audience, I don't necessarily disagree with this point. However, fitting the material available into the time allowed inevitably involves choices. If you are going to do some material on the 1970s TV show *Charlie's Angels*, for example, and the average age of your audience is middle-aged, they will usually 'get' the references without much explanation. A younger audience may not be quite so familiar with the original show and the characters, although they may have seen the more recent movie version with Drew Barrymore. Does this matter? Do you have to know the original series to get the jokes? Do you need to write some lines of explanation about what happened in the original show to make sure they get the jokes? Are the jokes strong enough to make it worthwhile having to use some of your time setting up the context? Obviously I can't answer those questions without knowing what you want to say about *Charlie's Angels* and which audience you want to say it to – but these are the types of questions you should be asking while working on a routine like this.

As discussed in our joke-writing chapter, it is also worth bearing in mind the tastes and boundaries of the audience to which you are playing, and of any company or network involved in broadcasting the show. You may still decide to push beyond those boundaries but at least if you do and there are objections it will be down to your deliberate choice (and hopefully one you are prepared to fight for) and not just because you didn't bother to find out ahead of time.

Point of view and purpose

The time and format requirements of the routine you are writing and the type of audience you are playing to are both important factors which may lead you to change or adapt your routine as you work on it. However our third consideration, your point of view, or the point of view of the performer you are writing for, is the factor which more than any other will turn your routine from a slightly mechanical 'construct jokes to order' process into something personal, exciting and unique.

Anyone who has been part of a debating team or has had to make a sales pitch knows that the main criterion for whether a joke or story ends up in the finished script is whether it fits with the overall purpose of the speech or routine itself.

In a comedy routine the 'purpose', besides entertaining the audience, is often to present the comic's unique point of view, and it is very important to be clear on what that point of view actually is when it comes to selecting material for them. For instance, a current popular theme in modern culture is the 'atheism versus spirituality' debate, and it is one that comics have been just as vocal on as everyone else.

As an illustration of how point of view can change the same basic joke material, Ricky Gervais attracted headlines in the USA with his controversial closing line while presenting an awards ceremony on national TV ('I'd like to thank God for making me an atheist'). The line reflected a point of view he has often drawn on for his stage shows. As a comedy writer who is also a Christian I may not personally agree with Ricky's philosophical position but I can certainly admire the energy and humour with which he presents it. In fact, as I sometimes tell my own audiences, poking fun at religion is definitely one of Ricky's God-given gifts. The basis of that line and Ricky's original line is virtually the same: both are simply variations of the 'opposite confirmation' type of joke we discussed back in Chapter Three.

It is just the point of view of the person telling them which determines which version of the joke fits better into which person's routine.

Most of us know without having to think too much about it what our current perspective on the big topics like religion or politics is. If we are writing for somebody else we can usually find out their take on the big subjects fairly easily too, either by discussing it with them or just by reviewing some of their previous routines.

For those topics in life on which you or the person you are writing for have not as yet identified any point of view, there are lots of commonly used techniques to discover one – from brainstorming to 'ranting' (simply speaking out loud for five or ten minutes on the topic without planning or restricting what you say), to getting friends or family to fire random questions at you either in person or by email to which you have to answer with the first thing that pops into your head.

Sometimes you'll end up with a point of view which is exactly what you thought it would be, but often the most interesting comedy comes from those points of view which emerge in the process and take you by surprise

Do note though that the 'not interested' point of view is still a usable point of view – in fact, much observational comedy comes from a performer 'exploring' topics out loud (although they are usually working in jokes they have thought of ahead of time). One of the UK's top female stand-ups, Angie Le Mar, when asked to contribute a routine on football to a sports-based show, responded with a very funny routine which began with explaining how, having no interest or knowledge of the sport itself, she has learned to identify football players from the shape of their calves.

In our last chapter we generated jokes based on a news story about somebody who had a tattoo. As you'll recall, we didn't really have a 'point of view' on tattoos or being tattooed beyond the fact that getting a wedding picture tattooed on yourself was a somewhat extreme, and therefore funny, thing to do.

Contrast this with the point of view of award-winning (and very tattooed) UK comedian Jim Smallman. Jim's first one-person show was an autobiographical one called 'The Boy Next Door Gone Wrong' which was a success on both sides of the Atlantic, but it was an audience response to his tattoos that gave him the idea for his next show:

'The idea to write a show based on my tattoos came from me working at a tattoo convention rather than a comedy club and having to explain the silly reasons behind them all the time. After that, I started writing more and more material. The idea behind "Tattooligan" is based on something that a woman in a supermarket said about me to her daughter over a year ago. She said to her little girl that "all people with tattoos are evil", so I thought I'd examine whether or not I am.

I sat down and tried to write as much material about my tattoos as possible – I've got seventeen in total, and already had strong material on five of them. I began to work on material on more of them that I could try out at previews of the show. This material is all linked together with stories about my life and giving the audience the chance to decide on my "is he/isn't he" evil hypothesis. The tattoo stuff is part of me, I'm covered in them – so there's some humour there but most of the humour comes from me going off on a tangent and relating other stories.

The "big reveal" at the end of my show is the real reasons behind my tattoos. I spend most of the show lampooning them and trying to insist that they're all silly and frivolous, but there are really deep personal reasons behind them and hopefully that helps wrap up my life story at the end of the show. It's a much more personal moment to end on, but there is of course a final twist!'

You'll have to book Jim (his website is www.jimsmallman.com) or track down a video of his show to find out what that twist is, but, as I am sure you can see, any jokes that Jim has about tattoos will be coming from a very different perspective from the ones a non-tattooed writer might produce from the outside looking in.

In terms of writing effective material and choosing what to leave out and what to put in for your own projects, point of view is both an effective trigger at the beginning and a good yardstick at the end. If something is very personal or emotive for you or for the person you write for, but your material on the subject is something anyone else could have written just as easily, you are probably not digging deep enough and very likely missing out on real comedy gold.

New material and special material

As well as complete routines, writers are sometimes asked to contribute special material to add to existing routines. I've already mentioned that from five-minute spots to full one-person shows the best comics and their writers should be constantly working to polish their performances and material throughout their career. Most good comics know this already and, like Jim Smallman, are writing and trying out new material all the time. Or, to put it more accurately, most sensible comics know that this is what they *should* be doing. The nature of new material, like all comedy, is that until it is performed in front of an audience, it is impossible to predict with any certainty whether or not it is going to work. While some well-known performers throw caution to the wind and perform large amounts of new material and sometimes entirely new shows in one go, most comics prefer to try smaller amounts of new stuff – sometimes just a new line or two – sandwiched between material that is already tried and tested.

As well as the jokes themselves, good linking lines to marry up the existing material with the new lines can be very useful and something a skilful writer can help with.

Having worked as a topical comedy writer for a long time, I am used to being approached by comics and speakers who are doing specific gigs such as charity or fundraising events or corporate shows for specific clients, as well as by performers who are due to take their shows overseas, to provide specially tailored material for those particular jobs.

It's surprising how just a few well-written lines which directly relate to the theme of a fundraising show or to the specific country or region the comedian is visiting can make their existing routine seem much fresher and more immediate.

I usually know very little about the cause or the country before I start working on this kind of job, which is where research on the internet or in the local library comes in handy. As always, I am looking not just for information on the topic itself but also current events which might be tied in with the topic. For instance, the English soccer team was going through (yet another) bad patch at the same time as I was producing material for the 'Let's Kick Racism Out of Football' campaign. Given that everybody at a fundraising show tends to be in agreement with the same point of view it is sometimes a good idea for a comic to make things feel less cosy by taking (or at least appearing to) the exact opposite point of view.

Putting these two ideas together resulted in the following line, which went down very well:

Kick Racism Out Of Football is a nice idea, but be honest, don't you get sick of all those foreign players coming over here with their disgusting and strange habits?

Such as winning . . .

As well as writing new material to order, it can be very useful to run through a performer's or speaker's existing material to see if any of it can be adapted to make it more relevant to a local audience, whether they are travelling overseas or just a bit further from their usual stamping ground than normal. Given that most of the comedy club circuit tends to be concentrated in a few of the larger cities, it is possible for a comic to get regular work for quite a long period without ever having to leave the city boundaries – but, from an artistic as well as a commercial point of view, it is much better to have an act that you know can travel.

As we mentioned in our previous chapter, politicians, sports people and local celebrities tend to behave, and misbehave, in similar ways wherever you go. It is usually not too difficult, once you have done a bit of research, to insert new names into your existing material on similar scandals and get the same laugh results. It makes sense, of course, to check what the local sense of humour is like. For example, English audiences usually take jokes about their own country in good part even when made by foreigners. Scottish and Irish audiences are fine with laughing at themselves too but can be a lot less willing to laugh when they perceive an outsider is poking fun at them.

Just as important as adding local references to material which is being taken on a trip is checking if there are any existing local references which might need to be modified. An example would be city-based comedians with a lot of material based on the frustrations of travelling on their local Underground or subway system. While it doesn't need to be dropped entirely – even people who have never been to a city are familiar with how the transport system works – very specific frustrations which only apply to regular commuters may have less relevance to audiences who only use the system when visiting.

Alternatively, identifying what the differences are between the visitor and the resident's experience may in itself be a good source of comedy ideas to amuse both parties.

Organising the routine

Once we know what kind of routine we are setting out to write and have tapped into whatever point of view we intend to write it from, it's time at last to apply our familiar brainstorming process to produce material to suit the theme, whether that material is in joke or story form.

Once that task is completed, the next step is to take the raw material we come up with and organise it into an actual routine. Although a routine may have one overall theme, which may be a particular topic or just the particular performer's persona and view of the world, as we progress beyond five- and ten-minute time slots into longer routines it is usually better, from both a writing point of view and an audience attention point of view, to break that overall topic into a serious of subtopics.

One of the first routines I worked on was about sugar levels, diabetes and related medical issues – perhaps not the most obviously amusing of themes. As it happens (and this was one of the reasons why I chose the topic) I have quite a lot of background knowledge on this medical condition drawn from personal experience as well as from involvement with one of the related charities. However, I also wanted to make the routine understandable to people who know very little about the subject. Having first applied the brainstorming process and breaking the overall topic down into potential areas for humour, the next step was to identify the ones which would make the most sense to the widest range of people. Childhood and schooldays seemed like a good place to start because even people who don't have personal experience of diabetes do have experience of being children and being at school:

Whenever my brother and I shared a packet of Polo mints he got all the mints and I just got the holes.

When our auntie came back from her holidays, his stick of rock said 'Blackpool' all the way through it – mine just said 'Don't even think about it'.

And so on. The 'universality' of schooldays and childhood means that many comedy routines, by comics of all shapes and ages, can get a lot of mileage out of this theme.

The two jokes above are also examples of ones which might need a bit of expansion or adaptation for overseas audiences. British audiences will recognise the brand name 'Polo' as relating to round mint-flavoured sweets with holes in the middle. In the USA 'Lifesavers' would be the brand that conjures the same image. It might also be possible to rejig the joke to feature ring-shaped doughnuts for countries which don't have either brand of candy. (Thanks to Homer Simpson, there are very few places in the world where people don't know what doughnuts look like!)

For the second joke, rather than changing the subject matter,

113

as then the joke wouldn't make any sense at all, it would probably be best for a comedian playing to an overseas audience to
simply fill them in beforehand on the fact that the traditional
gift brought back from British seaside resorts is a 'stick of rock'
– a long baton-shaped sweet with the name of the resort printed
through the middle.

Not everything in a comedy routine needs to be a 'joke'.
Indeed many comedians' styles are 'story' rather than joke-based.
The stories can be real ones – after all, life is often funnier than
anything you can make up – and even if the story is a basically
mundane one, the art of the storyteller can still make it entertaining. In many routines the stories are usually 'real' in that
they are based on something which has actually happened to the
comic but the details of the story have usually been tweaked to
make it more comedic.

> I once had a hypoglycaemic attack when I was on a train. But
> people didn't know it was a drop in blood sugar – they thought
> I was an epileptic. And the one thing everybody 'knows' about
> epilepsy is that you are supposed to stick a pen under the
> person's tongue to reduce the chances of them swallowing it.

> It *does* reduce the chances of them swallowing their tongue –
> because they'll be too busy choking on your ballpoint.

So far the story is one that could easily happen and one which
everybody can relate to, both the unfortunate people who may
have become ill in public and the rest of us who will probably at
some point have been in a situation where somebody around us
became ill and we wondered what to do. (On that point, please
note that people with epilepsy *do not* swallow their tongues and
the 'pen' technique is a dangerous urban myth!)

Using this kind of real-life experience and then adding some
imagination can take the material in more surreal directions:

> What really worries me is the fact that these days not everyone
> uses pen and paper when they are travelling. A lot of people

use laptops and smart phones. Now I'm scared that next time I have an attack people will be sticking their iPad down my neck.

Still – an Apple a day keeps the doctor away.

Silly jokes like this last one often pop up when you are brainstorming topics based on real-life stories and have moved beyond the real-life possibilities. As we have already noted, you can't necessarily get a whole routine out of pun-based jokes (unless you are the brilliant UK comic Tim Vine who specialises in them) but unexpectedly dropping in one like the above 'groaner' at the end of a realistic story can catch the audience off guard and lead to very big laughs. In fact the more stand-up comedy you watch, the more you'll note that once a comedian starts to get very, very deadpan, serious and even dark, there is often a very silly gag lurking just round the corner to break the tension.

When incorporating a 'true story' of your own into a routine (or working on one with the performer it happened to), your job as a writer is to find ways of telling the story that are interesting and amusing to everyone who wasn't there.

I have often found that the best way to work with performers on this kind of material is simply to have them tell the story from start to finish without necessarily trying to make it funny. While taking notes (or even recording the chat) you can then ask the questions that draw out further details to give you a lot more material to rewrite the story with its full comic potential.

There is another advantage to working this way. While we can sometimes decide that personal stories of our own are more relevant to other people than they actually are, the opposite can also be true. In discussing comedians' 'big stories' for their routines, I have sometimes stumbled on small details and related experiences which they wouldn't normally have mentioned as they may feel they are too boring or too personal to be of general interest. It often transpires that these bits of 'truth' become the funniest parts of the routine and get bigger laughs than whatever comic incident triggered the story in the first place.

Remember that different people respond to information in different ways. Some people really like words and how they sound, so simply telling the story in clever, evocative language will 'tickle' them. Others are more visual, so when the comedian tells the story and actually acts out the way he or she was behaving and demonstrates some of the reactions of the other people, that is what will really get visual people chuckling. Still others of us are very 'feeling' orientated, so the fastest way to our funny bone will be emphasising the feelings the participants in any story experience. For maximum effect try to include visual, aural and emotive elements in all your material and, in theory, you should make everyone happy.

A strong opening

We've suggested that one of the comedy writer's jobs is to make the scary business of making people laugh a bit less scary for the performer. Nowhere else is this service more relevant than at the start of a comedy routine. Even the most seasoned and successful acts will admit to being slightly nervous when they hear their name being called and they have to take that long, lonely walk to the microphone stand. What inexperienced performers and public speakers sometimes don't understand is that the audience is just as apprehensive as they are. After all, in coming out for the evening, they have already invested precious time they are not ever going to get back, and they have also invested money in booking their seats, paying for drinks and food and often expensive parking fees too. So if the audience members are not entertained, not only is all that money wasted, but their judgement in choosing to spend it on this event is also called into question.

Taking all that into account, it is easy to see why the average audience is just as keen for the routine to go well as the comic. (It also explains why audiences who have got in for free or who have been 'forced' to sit through your act at a corporate show can be among the toughest crowds to handle.)

Certainly comedy audiences in some of the top clubs can be

very demanding and comics who don't meet their high standards may get heckled off – but seeing a comic 'die' on stage really isn't what they want. There will, of course, always be one or two people who think they are funnier than the comic (more about them later) but in general when the audience as a whole starts heckling or shouting it is out of embarrassment and disappointment more than aggression. An act which isn't going well is embarrassing for everybody, and the instinctive reaction is to want it to end as quickly as possible and by any means possible.

The best way to dispel fears of anything embarrassing happening in the minds of both the performer and the audience is to make sure the routine has a strong opening with a good strong laugh line sooner rather than later. That's why comics and writers will invest a lot of time in trying out opening lines and ways to get on stage which work best for that particular performer. It's also why when they hit on an opener that works it often remains part of the act no matter how much updating and changing the rest of the routine goes through.

For many comedians their standard opening line becomes so familiar that it eventually becomes their 'catchphrase', be it Sir Bruce Forsyth's 'Nice to see you, to see you nice' or Rodney Dangerfield's 'I don't get no respect . . .' Whether rightly or wrongly, good jokes from almost any comedian or speaker's act can be borrowed and adapted by other performers but it is very hard to do this with somebody else's opening line. That's because the ideal opening line not only gets a laugh but is tied very tightly to the persona of the comedian it relates to.

While waiting to develop that ideal opener – and it often takes a lot of trial and error – it certainly makes sense that in the meantime whatever material you put at the top of the routine is drawn from your strongest stuff. It may take two or three jokes to get people laughing but once that initial laugh comes it makes a big difference to everyone. The comic gets a confidence boost and the audience gets confirmation that they are not about to witness a 'car crash' but can relax and hand the responsibility for creating good times over to somebody who obviously knows what they are doing.

As stand-ups progress through their careers they often develop their own collection of 'bankers'. These are the jokes that, insofar as it is ever possible in comedy, they can 'bank on' to get them a laugh in almost every circumstance. While beginners may need to use all of their 'bankers' at the beginning of their routine to ensure they get that first vital laugh, as comics develop more material and more confidence they often keep some of those sure-fire jokes in reserve for times when something doesn't work and they need to get the routine back on track. If things are really going downhill, they can pull out their 'emergency gags', get at least one laugh and then say goodnight and leave the stage.

What happens after the opening depends very much on the persona of the individual performer. Some comedians stick very closely to their script, without much interaction with the audience. Others are much more conversational – chatting to the people in the front row and generally playing around before they get into previously written material. However, even with this approach, some performers are more comfortable and less rehearsed than others. I have sometimes sat with comics and helped them brainstorm jokes based on every possible answer to questions like 'So where do you come from?' and 'What do you do for a living?' Personally, I'd rather the comics found more original questions to ask – both of those old chestnuts have become comedy clichés. Nine times out of ten, no matter how many answers you rehearse the chances are the audience member you pick on will come up with the one you didn't think of. The good news is that faced with an answer they haven't rehearsed a joke for, the comic will often come up with a response that is better than anything they had prepared. Questions are just one way of connecting with an audience early in the routine. Another way is to get them to physically do something such as putting their hands up in response to a 'how many people' type of survey. It's the comedy equivalent of a hip hop artist telling the audience to say 'Yo!' and is actually a very old theatrical technique. Get an audience to do something at your command and you have established that you are in charge.

Links and variety

As the time allocated to the routine you are working on gets longer, there is scope for more topics to be covered between the beginning and the end. Indeed, it is often a good idea to build in some variety even if the overall theme of your routine is a very consistent one. Just as with a sitcom or movie with a strong main plot, the occasional change of scene or subplot tends to enhance and add an extra dimension, rather than diminishing the main thrust of the piece. This being the case, you will want to create good link material to get from one topic to the other and back again if you need to. Sometimes the topics you cover in your routine will be very closely related and sometimes they will be more tangential.

At the time I was working on the routine about diabetes, the other big thing going on in my life was the imminent arrival of my first (and, as it has turned out, only) son. Just like school days, the advent of parenting and especially the differences between male and female attitudes to pregnancy are common experiences for many people and as a result good sources of potential comedy material. As with school days, the universality of the subject means that the big challenge is finding a comedy angle which hasn't been done to death already.

I'd love to say that linking diabetes to pregnancy was my way of breaking new comedy ground, but the truth is that like a lot of males, becoming a parent was something I had never given much thought to until it actually happened to me. Once it did, I wanted to talk about it to anyone who would listen, and that included any comedy audiences I happened to find myself in front of.

So having decided to go from one topic to the other, what could I use to link them? Although some fast-talking comics can pull off switching abruptly from one topic to a completely different one with no connection at all, for most of us there needs to be a transition of some sort. I definitely wanted to avoid the kind of contrived link along the lines of 'being addicted to sugar sure is tough, baby . . . and speaking of babies . . .', which only works if you are deliberately parodying bad comics or presenters.

The solution is usually to study the two topics you want to link together from every angle until you can find something they genuinely have in common, or alternatively some way in which they are opposites. In my case the one common problem that struck me about diabetes and pregnancy, which anyone who has either condition will back me up on, is the need to go to the toilet more often than would normally be the case. From there I started off by talking about the difficulties of constantly needing the toilet in city centres, but finding that the only option available is usually one of those expensive bars or restaurants with the warning signs about toilets being 'for customers only'. Not being brave enough to sneak in and use the toilet regardless, I therefore have to buy lots of drinks I don't want just so I can use the facilities. Which means that five minutes after I come out of one bar, I'm desperate to find another so I can use the toilet again.

In telling this story, I can then reveal that according to my research there is an ancient by-law in London which gives pregnant women the right to go the toilet anywhere – a public building, a private building, even in the street without fear of prosecution. This leads me into the story of the assistant manager who tried to stop an expectant mother using the toilet in his pub: she tried to argue with him but eventually she had to go over his head.

And with that tasteful anecdote I have now moved smoothly from the subject of diabetes to the subject of parenthood and my material on the latter theme can continue from there for as long as I want it to. (Incidentally, I don't know if that pregnancy by-law exists in any other city besides London, or indeed if it is still in force – so if you do happen to be expecting at the moment, please don't take advantage of it purely on my say-so and then blame me if you get arrested.)

Reincorporation

As well as directly linking from topic to topic, a very useful technique for weaving the different strands of your routine together, and giving a sense of completion and closure to the journey from your opening joke to your 'big finish' is the use of 'reincorporation' or the 'callback' as it is also known. This is a technique that will be very familiar to film fans, and simply means reintroducing or 'calling back' a character, line or subject which you referred to earlier in your routine, preferably in an unexpected, creative and amusing way.

If you haven't seen the James Bond movie *Live and Let Die*, look away now as I am about to reveal the ending to demonstrate the basic idea of a 'callback'.

At the movie's climax our hero and his lady friend are tied to a metal frame which is about to be dropped into a pool of crocodiles by the main villain. However, what the evil Mr Big doesn't realise is that Bond is wearing his trusty magnetic watch which he uses to attract some explosive pellets that the bad guy happens to have left lying round his lair. Needless to say, at the very last minute 007 manages to escape, using the explosives to dispatch the bad guy and save the day. What makes the audience smile is that, unlike Mr Big, we all knew he had a magnetic watch. It's just that we had forgotten all about it because it was introduced almost two hours earlier in a comedy sequence at the beginning of the movie which, until the end, seemed totally unconnected to the main plot. I'm sure you can think of countless other examples of this kind of 'callback' in movies both comedic and dramatic.

A dialogue-based example occurs in David Schwimmer's film comedy *Run Fatboy Run*, when Whit, the arrogant businessman (played by Hank Azaria) who is Simon Pegg's rival for the affections of his ex-partner Libby, is showing off his flashy remote-controlled sailboat to Jake, their young son.

Naturally Jake asks if he can have a go. 'No – but you can watch me control it' is Whit's selfish response.

Later, having failed in his attempt to cheat in the movie's climactic marathon race, Whit is confined to a hospital bed. As he tries to justify his actions to an angry Libby, young Jake is making his discomfort worse by constantly adjusting and re-adjusting the electronic bed. His response to Whit's exasperated instruction to hand over the remote? You guessed it: 'No – but you can watch me control it.'

As we already know, our brain loves patterns so when we recognise a line or an incident that we remember from earlier, and realise it has now been given a different significance or meaning, we laugh with delight not only at the cleverness of the writer but also at our own cleverness in spotting the connection.

Of course, like all successful 'magic' the trick isn't as difficult to achieve as it looks. In one of my own routines I tell a somewhat exaggerated but basically true story about my father, who worked for the Irish lighthouse service. This often meant spending weeks and months on remote islands where, in the days before video and DVD, the only entertainment available was a nightly boat trip to the mainland to the town's one and only cinema.

As the cinema didn't change its programme very often, my father and his shipmates probably hold the world record for sitting through the same movie (*Invasion of the Body Snatchers*, in case you're interested) more nights in a row than any other seafarers in history.

Much later in the routine, there is some material about being bullied at school, and in the course of it, I share with the audience how supportive my father was. With inspiring words he told me to always hold on to what I believed no matter how many people told me I was wrong.

'Is that something your own father told you?' I asked him.

'No – it's a line from *Invasion of the Body Snatchers*.

Of course that's not exactly what he said, and nor is it a direct quote from the movie, but bringing the movie title back in at the point where people have virtually forgotten it almost always results in a big laugh and, occasionally, even a round of applause.

As you will probably have guessed, this effect is achieved in exactly the same way as it would be in a movie. Just like a movie script, you don't need to write your comedy routine in the same order you are going to perform it.

When I was brainstorming ideas for the routine beforehand, I jotted down the lighthouse story completely separately from the bullying material, and it was only in playing around with potential links, ideas and connections that I spotted the two ideas could be linked together. Sometimes creating a callback is done even more mechanically. Just as in the joke technique where we think of a punchline and then create a feed line to make it funny, if we have a particularly significant story or turn of phrase we know we are going to include at the end of our routine, it usually isn't difficult to find a way to use the same phrase or idea in a low-key way earlier in the routine, to set up the bigger laugh for later.

I suspect that the James Bond scriptwriters worked the same way: first coming up with the 'magnetic watch' idea as a means of escaping the trap at the end of the movie, and only then thinking of ways to introduce the idea of the watch earlier in the script.

Because these backwards and forwards links are so useful when polishing routines, not to mention the comedy scripts we will be looking at in the next chapter, I am a great believer, even in these technological times, in jotting down my initial ideas and blocks of material on old-fashioned index cards that I can physically shuffle and move around before committing them to the computer screen. It can make the connections easier to spot.

As with all of our comedy techniques, do practise this one in your own writing, but do also remember to use it sparingly so that it doesn't get to the point that the audience starts to spot elements of your routine which are very obviously being introduced in the beginning for no other reason than to be brought back later. People are much easier to surprise when they don't know they are being set up.

Well, at least that's what happens in *Invasion of the Body Snatchers*.

The big finish

Whether your routine or speech has lasted five minutes or two hours, all good things must come to an end. Hopefully, your audience will also agree that your routine has been a good thing.

In addition to the practical considerations of sticking to your allotted time and increasing your chances of getting rebooked, there is also a very wise old showbusiness adage to 'always leave them wanting more'.

As with other elements of comedy, the accepted way of getting off stage varies from comedian to comedian. Some comics go for the very traditional method of finishing with a song, either comedy-based or, if the act is particularly traditional, a sentimental one. (You may be surprised at how many popular musical 'standards' were originally written for and launched by comedians.) Another 'mechanical' way to signal the end of a routine is with a humorous poem or a clever quote either of the comic's own invention or borrowed from somebody else. 'Remember, folks, laughter is the best medicine, unless you are diabetic, in which case insulin is pretty high on the list' has become one such classic line, originally attributed to British comedian Jasper Carrott.

A word of caution though. This is certainly a brilliant gag, which is why it has been 'adapted', 'borrowed' or stolen outright by countless comics and speakers. A great line like this will still get you a laugh if you use it as your own closer, even if many of us have heard it before. What it won't get you is the reputation for being original, which is so vital to advancing your career in the comedy market. When other comedians start stealing *your* lines, you will know you are getting somewhere.

As we have discussed above, another way to bring your routine to a close is by calling back or reincorporating some or all of the various topics you have touched on over the course of the routine. If you can find a way to bring together a number of seemingly unconnected threads at the end, it not only creates a sense of satisfaction and closure for the audience but also does you no harm at all in your goal to be recognised as a clever and original writer.

I should also note that several comedians who regularly play the comedy circuit, either as part of a varied bill or as headliners in their own right, don't necessarily have an 'ending' for their act. They just tell their last gag, make a 'that's all from me' type statement and walk to the wings. This can work well for performers who have an 'ordinary person who happens to have stepped up to the mike' persona. In most cases though, 'being ordinary' on stage is an illusion which usually requires a lot of stage time and experience to create and sustain. There is also the standard 'alternative comedian' sign-off – 'I've been Joe Bloggs, you've been great . . .', which may have sounded fresh in the 1980s but is now almost as much of a comedy cliché as finishing with a song and dance.

As with the best opening line for you or the person you write for, the best closing line will be dictated by what kind of comedian you are, what kind of material you do and, not least, the response you get from the audiences on which you try out your various prospective closing lines.

In the 'stand-up cartooning' show I do for children and families, which involves being on stage with a large drawing board, I found that the best closing lines were the ones which not only linked the kind of act I was doing, but also addressed the practical issue of getting me and the drawing board off stage in often cramped venues without injuring anyone:

> Ladies and gentlemen, one of the greatest moments in an artist's career is when they bring an audience to their feet. Some people do it with the strength of their performance. Some do it with the quality of their material.
>
> I'm going to do it by running straight at you with this large, heavy piece of wood . . .

My favourite closing line is one from Gene Perret, the distinguished American comedy writer who was one of the first to demystify and share many of the comedy writing techniques we have been discussing in this book. It goes something like this:

> If you can make just one person laugh, if you only get one smile, if you can make only one person happy . . .
>
> then you know your act stinks!

Timing, rhythm and attitude

As we have been working our way through the mechanics of putting together a comedy routine or speech, we have been concentrating on words and ideas. However, as we are writing material intended for performance, there are other elements which also need to be kept in mind, and which are a little harder to communicate via the pages of a book. Timing, rhythm, accent and the persona of the person we are writing for (whether that person is ourselves or somebody else) are all factors that will have an influence on how our material comes across to the audience, so it is important to consider them when we are writing our material in the first place.

At the start of the book, we noted that the one thing comedians and comedy writers don't always have a sense of humour about is comedy itself, but there are certainly some very old and traditional jokes about the business of comedy which every professional is familiar with, and one of the oldest is frequently told by comedy double acts. It involves one person asking the question 'What is the secret of comedy?' and the other person answering 'Timing' before the first has finished speaking.

Actually good timing is a skill every speaker and performer needs to be aware of but it is one which is absolutely essential for a comedian, whether working solo or with a partner. The right pause just before a punchline can make the joke much stronger, the wrong gap or pause can kill it stone dead. Leave too long a gap and the audience may work out the 'twist' in the ending before you reveal it. Come in too quickly with the punchline and the audience may not have time to make the connection in their heads to 'get' whatever clever wordplay or mental picture makes your joke work. And of course when your first joke does work, you need to know how much time to leave for the audience to finish laughing so that they don't miss the set-up to your next piece of material.

There are only two ways to learn comedy timing – the first way is to study as many of the great comics and speakers as you can and try to work out the 'secret' of each individual's approach to timing. You'll find there is a lot of variation with the only constant being that each performer has a style that works for them. The second way is to get practising. You may or may not get it right at first, but you will start to get a feel for what works for you and for the people you write for. Once you do get that idea clearer it will help you write material that works well with the timing of the person performing it, and will also give you clues on how to adjust the timing of particular pieces of material that don't seem to be working. Sometimes fixing the timing is the key to making good material work rather than having to delete it from the routine altogether.

A similar process applies to working with rhythm. We all have a natural rhythm of speech, sometimes derived from our personality and often influenced by our native accent and the communication style of the family or environment we grew up in. The same is true of performers, some of whom speak with a similar rhythm when they are on stage, and some who, either deliberately or instinctively, become a more exaggerated version of themselves when they step into the spotlight. Many comedians adopt a 'speak fast and then slow, speak fast and then slow' type of rhythm which seems to lend itself to set-ups and punchlines, while other comedians aim for a rising inflection, which is almost a 'mini laugh' when they deliver the punchline of each joke. Listen to a selection of stand-up routines and you will start to recognise it. Your task as a writer is to listen to the individual you are writing for, get familiar with their rhythm and give them material that works with it rather than against it.

Incidentally, some of the most famous comedians are known not just for their catchphrases but also for the little 'verbal tics' that punctuate their act. The British comedian Frankie Howerd always made lots of 'oohs and aahs' as he told his gags, which accentuated the air of 'naughtiness' lurking just below the surface of his material. Eddie Izzard's material frequently has a somewhat vague and almost mumbling quality just before he launches into a completely unexpected and usually hilarious detour from whatever topic he has just been talking about. The overall effect enhances even further the sense that Izzard's material is being created there and then and right before our eyes. In Howerd's case it has now entered comedy folklore that the 'oohs' and 'aahs' didn't naturally occur in performance and were actually written into each script. It wouldn't surprise me to learn that in the early stages of the comedian's career they probably did appear instinctively and were then adopted by the comic and his writers as something worth intentionally developing. Rowan Atkinson, who has played a wide range of memorable characters from Mr Bean to Blackadder, has a particularly distinctive way of pronouncing the letter 'B', and writers on projects he has appeared in have often used this to advantage by ensuring that character names like 'Bob' and 'Bough' make regular appearances.

Using visuals, facial expressions and gestures is another way in which a comedian's presentation can add something to your scripted words. We discussed in the last chapter how different aspects of a presentation – visual, verbal or emotional – appeal to different members of the audience. American comedy legend George Burns was still performing at 100 years old – and still smoking ten to fifteen cigars a day. However, his cigar also played a part in his comedy delivery, the rhythm of putting it in his mouth, inhaling, taking it out, becoming part of the rhythm of his delivery, enhancing the sense of his being a wise and witty 'elder statesman of comedy' whose lines were well worth taking time to savour. One of the most inventive of modern stand-up comedians and one whose humour appeals to audiences around the world, Australia's Jimeoin does some very funny material on how simply raising or lowering the eyebrows when using everyday phrases can completely change their meaning, and this is just as true for comedians as it is for the rest of us.

It also reminds me to remind you that as a writer you need to be aware of the context in which your material is going to be delivered. A facial gesture, raising an eyebrow, displaying a magazine or book cover – there are lots of visual things you can build into a routine to enhance its appeal, but it is important to make sure that those elements work as well for the person at the back of the venue as they do for the person in the front row. In a small comedy club, on a TV show or even in large stadium with video screens, tiny gestures can get big laughs. In a larger venue without screens, or one which is an unusual shape, or where people are eating as well as watching the show, they can often be missed. If this happens once or twice it isn't a problem, but an act which relies very heavily on this style of presentation may need some more focused reworking if it is being performed outside its usual context. There are other issues which affect timing and delivery depending on the context of the show: when a show is being filmed live but designed for broadcast, comedians often use the mantra 'deliver the set-up lines to the studio audience and the punchline to camera'.

If you can track down a DVD of one of your favourite comics and an audio recording of the same routine (I mean as a different product, not just the audio track from the DVD), it is a good learning experience to listen to the audio first and then watch the DVD. Is there anything on the DVD which didn't work or make sense when you listened to the audio version? It may also be that you notice material on the DVD which was obviously edited out of the audio version precisely because it made no sense without the pictures. As a writer, making adaptations to material for practical reasons as well as comedic ones is very much part of your job.

The attitude or tone with which a comedian delivers material is another element that has an effect on how it comes across, and this is something the writer needs to be aware of at the initial stages. For instance a comic doing 'heavy' material on topics such as racism, homelessness, sexuality or disability may deliberately adopt a very 'lighthearted' style which, depending on the comic, either allows them to say something the audience might not normally be comfortable to hear in a more palatable way, or alternatively shocks the audience into laughing by treating something we are 'not supposed to laugh about' in a way that makes us do just that. However, comics who are using material which is quite obviously fantasy based, whether telling us about crocodiles walking into bars or getting spectacularly and hilariously irate about some entirely trivial issue like Tom Hanks's haircut in *The Da Vinci Code*, often find that communicating something silly with the passion and gravitas normally reserved for matters of life-altering importance triggers the laughter response much more powerfully than if the lighthearted material was thrown away with the lightness it actually deserves.

One last element to be aware of in terms of writing for an individual is their particular vocal strengths and weaknesses. Just as you wouldn't write a song which ended on a very high note for a singer whose talents lie at the other end of the vocal register, it makes sense to work with rather than against vocal characterisation. As with Rowan Atkinson's 'B' words, when cartoon characters like Elmer Fudd or real-life performers with a similar tendency to replace 'R' with 'W' are given scripts, the chances are there will be more rather than fewer 'R' words in them to deliberately bring out that distinctive pronunciation.

However, as rhythm and timing are so important for effective comedy, what we don't want is the performer getting *accidentally* tripped up by particular words and phrases. It makes sense to know what those potential minefields are for the individual and work around them. In my own case, I have a slight stammer which tends to become a bit more pronounced when I am speaking in public and particularly trips me up on the letter 'L'. In the same way that Bob Hope made close friend Bing Crosby the frequent butt of his jokes, and Britain's foremost comedy duo Morecambe and Wise directed much of their friendly ribbing at popular singer Des O'Connor, the very successful Irish entertainer Daniel O'Donnell is often a target of homegrown humour. In my case I would need to steer well clear of Daniel jokes. This is not because I don't think he would take them in good part – although I don't know him personally, I do know that, like Bing and Des, not only can he take a joke but he can often come back with an even better one – but simply because the combination of several 'L's in his name means I always come out with something like 'DaniellODonnelllmpf' or something equally unintelligible. (And yes, you're right – I wouldn't include the word 'unintelligible' in my routine for exactly the same reason!)

Stand and deliver?

As I explained earlier, even though there are many excellent performers who also write, the book is very much written from the writer's perspective. With this in mind, the exercises you'll find at the end of this chapter relate to writing rather than performing routines.

As with all the exercises, I can't reach out of the page and make you do them, but I do think you'll get the best out of this book if you do the 'homework' for yourself.

However, there is one further exercise which I personally think is one of the most important in the book, but which I am aware may not be possible for everyone. I am therefore putting it in at this point as an optional task.

If you are already a performer or speaker you are no doubt already doing it (in which case please use the writing exercises as a challenge to work in a different style from your own natural one), but if you are purely a writer, and can't see yourself standing up to perform in a million years, I would very much like to encourage you to try it anyway, at least once.

Having worked as a writer and script editor for a wide range of talented performers and comics, I know at first hand how a great performer can add the emotion, panache, timing and all the other indefinable elements we have been talking about in this chapter to the words I have written and lift them from good to great. But no matter how much we study speakers, watch comedians and even work directly with performers on a one-to-one basis, the only way we writers can really get a 'feel' for how words on a page translate to words which are performed is to get up and perform something for ourselves.

You don't necessarily need to go the whole hog and book yourself an open mike spot in the roughest comedy club in town – although if you apply the advice in the last chapter about constructing jokes and the tips in this chapter for weaving them into a routine, you should be able to cobble together a routine that may not set the world on fire first time out but won't disgrace you either.

You may, however, prefer to work on a talk for your local church or a speech for an upcoming social function, join a debating society or start a public-speaking course. There are also stand-up comedy and improvisation classes which constantly spring up in community and adult education centres, many of which end in a 'showcase' performance for family and friends.

The important thing is that somehow, somewhere, you put yourself in a position where you have to get up in front of an audience of some sort and see what happens when you deliver your own material. Once you have done that, it doesn't matter whether your routine or speech succeeds, falls flat or blows the room away. What does matter is that you will get a much better sense of what is needed at the writing stage to translate into audience laughter and performer confidence at the delivery stage.

Some comedy writing teachers say that once you have had this experience you will never knowingly send a performer out to face an audience with material which is not your best. I prefer to believe that you wouldn't do this anyway. What performing yourself will give you, besides a respect for the importance of good material, is a better understanding of where the performers you will be writing for are coming from when they ask for changes in a word or a line, or for a better joke. You don't necessarily always have to agree to those changes, of course (well, not unless the performer has the power to get you fired), but having been in that position yourself even once or twice will help you make the call as to whether the writing, the performing or both need attention.

Even if your writing aspirations lean more towards sitcoms, sketches or other more ensemble-based forms of comedy, it is still a useful experience to have to deliver some words on stage for yourself. And assuming that doing so doesn't end up with you abandoning the writing side of your career due to a meteoric rise to fame in the stand-up spotlight, we'll turn our attention to these other types of comedy writing in our next chapter.

Over to you . . .

1 Identify a contemporary comic or speaker that you like and watch them do ten to twenty minutes of their act on TV, DVD or online. (You can go to see them live, of course, but unless you are good at note-taking it may prove difficult to remember the routine in detail, and recording it is liable to breach the rules of the venue.) Now let's assume they have been asked for a further five minutes of material to extend their routine. It will be your job to write this material in the style of the performer you have identified.

2 Take the same material you have written for Exercise 1 and rewrite it for two more comedians of your choice, each of whom should be very different in style from your original subject.

3 Write your own five-minute comedy routine, speech or presentation. If you do perform it as suggested earlier, try to get a recording of the routine. Rewrite it based on where you got laughs and where you didn't. Then perform it again. Rewrite it based on the response to your second attempt. Try the new rewrite in front of an audience . . . I think by now you get the idea of how to proceed with this exercise. 'Writing is rewriting' is an adage that every screenwriter takes to heart – and for the comedy writer, the write-perform-rewrite cycle is an ongoing part of the job, whether you ever set foot on stage in person or not.

5

Sketches, Sitcoms and Scripted Comedy

Many books and courses on sketch and sitcom writing begin with the warning to 'throw away your joke books'. I wouldn't quite agree with this. The purpose of sketches and sitcoms, just as much as stand-up routines, is to make us laugh and an understanding of joke structures will help a lot in achieving this. But it is certainly true that to write good sketches, sitcoms and other effective script-based comedy, you will need to do a little bit more than just string a lot of jokes together.

If you need proof of this fact, simply take a look at the string of cheaply produced 'parody' movies which have been released to cash in on the summer market over recent years. Or rather, take a look at one of them, and if you can stay awake till the end you deserve some sort of medal. *Epic Movie*, *Disaster Movie*, *Dance Movie*, *Superhero Movie* and their like usually consist of a series of sketches based on the best-known scenes from whatever movies of the title genre have been released in the previous twelve months, featuring lookalike actors, costumes and sets. Being aimed principally at the teenage market, the humour is usually very broad and crude, involves sex, violence or both with an extra topping of 'gross-out' humour.

While there are usually one or two visual gags in each movie which do work well, there are rarely enough to sustain the full movie running time. In fact a common complaint, even from the target audience of teenagers, is that the best jokes in these movies are usually contained in the movie trailers and the rest is just padding. Contrast this with *The Naked Gun* movies, the best of Mel Brooks's movies or even the original Wayans brothers' *Scary Movie* which started the parody craze. These movies feature exactly the same irreverent and sometimes gross humour as the teen-orientated ones. However, they also contain believable characters and a plot which works on its own merits rather than being simply an excuse to shoehorn lots of unrelated sketches together.

In your own sketch and sitcom writing it is also the elements of believability, characterisation and some logical connection to reality, even if it is a comedy version of reality, which will make the difference between work which might get a laugh or two simply for being topical, and work which will still be getting laughs long after it was originally written.

Sketching out ideas

Sitcoms by their nature are longer term projects, and even at very basic level require some degree of budget, whether the money is coming from you or from a production company. We will be looking at sitcom writing later in the chapter, but even if sitcom is your main goal there are very good reasons for trying your hand at sketch writing also.

For one thing, many top comedy writers and performers who are now well known for sitcom and movie projects first made their name in sketch comedy shows (even *The Simpsons* made their first appearance in short spots on *The Tracey Ullman Show*). More to the point, whether on the live comedy scene, in 'test' runs on TV and radio or in the ever-expanding world of online comedy, short quickies and sketches are one of the best and most affordable ways for aspiring writers and performers to establish themselves with both the comedy audience and the comedy industry.

As with any other form of comedy, the best first step to deciding which kind of sketch comedy you are going to turn your hand to is to take a quick overview of what has gone before and what is happening now. A search of YouTube or other internet video portals will come up with a wide range of successful sketches from the past including classic pieces from *Monty Python's Flying Circus*, *Laugh-In*, *Saturday Night Live* or *The Fast Show*. In many of these cases you'll find accompanying comments such as 'My all-time favourite sketch' or 'Still makes me laugh every time I see it', which just confirm that great sketch comedy is still great comedy years after the original sketch was written and performed. On newer sites such as Will Ferrell's 'Funny or Die' you can view a wide range of contemporary comedy, some of it made by working professionals, but much of it uploaded by up-and-coming comics and writers hoping to make a good first impression.

On the live comedy circuit, and especially at festivals, you will also find many sketch groups, some composed of members of the same drama school or college society, but many comprising a number of aspiring comedy writers and performers with not much more in common than a similar sense of humour and the ability to keep to the commitment of turning up to rehearsals on time.

Whether broadcast or live sketch comedy is your main aim, you will not by now be surprised to hear that the next step, having done your research, is to start brainstorming ideas for your sketch material. In some cases, such as with a regular topical sketch show, there will already be a clear brief for the kind of sketches required. One such live show called 'Newsrevue' has been running in London on a weekly basis for many years. In other cases, such as TV shows built around particular lead performers, the sketches required will obviously be of the kind which work well with that particular performer's individual strengths, or if they already have a gallery of regular characters, sketches which will allow those characters to do their stuff.

By now you should be a seasoned brainstormer, but let's quickly take the subject of 'jobs' and probe it for sketch ideas. What kind of jobs have you done in the past? Include part-time jobs, summer jobs, household chores – even fantasy jobs count while brainstorming. What funny incidents happened to you while doing those jobs? What not-so-funny incidents happened that you could make funny with a bit of hindsight and exaggeration? Remember, Woody Allen famously defined comedy as 'tragedy plus time'. Who would have been the most inappropriate person to have been doing your job? Celebrities are always popular characters to place in unusual jobs, and as anyone who watches topical comedy shows knows, if the concept of the sketch is funny enough, the characterisation of the celebrity doesn't need to be picture perfect. As already noted, if there is a particular comic or actor with an existing range of comedy characters, you might want to explore which jobs those characters could be given which would enable them to display their unique comedy traits.

As evidenced by the type of parody movies we were talking about earlier, another easy route to sketch ideas is to apply the 'What if?' process to ideas and scenes we are already familiar with. Movie or classic historical scenes are particular favourites for this kind of approach – we have all seen or read about the original so we know what's supposed to happen, which makes it easy to generate laughs by having something unexpected happen instead. An iconic movie like *Casablanca* can be parodied over and over again in sketch comedy, and the result will be different every time depending on the comedians or performers who take the lead roles. In the case of *Casablanca*, parody versions have included a sketch by the largely black cast of *In Living Color* (a very cutting-edge show in the 1990s) which hinged on the then widespread practice of 'colourising' classic movies for cable television. This version of *Casablanca* replaced Humphrey Bogart with actor Billy Dee Williams in what the show called a '*very* colourised' version of the movie, complete with Stevie Wonder playing the piano in Rick's Bar. *Sesame Street*'s version of *Casablanca* also focused on the bar scene – in this case the song lyric 'A kiss is just a kiss' was transformed into 'an S is just an S' in line with the show's genius for combining education with entertainment. Play the scene in your own head and 'cast' comedy characters of your own choice in the lead roles, and it is easy to see how they would change the familiar movie moments into something new. If Courtney Cox in 'Monica from *Friends*' mode played the Ingrid Bergman part it might be very hard to get her onto the plane at the film's climax without a very detailed check of the flight safety arrangements, while replacing Bogart with John Cleese as Basil Fawlty would no doubt mean that Sam was given a comprehensive Manuel-the-waiter-style slapping before he ever got a chance to 'Play it Again'.

At the other end of the scale from classic black-and-white movies are the bright and shiny worlds of children's TV and television advertising, but these areas too are often fertile fields from which comedy writers can derive sketch ideas. British comedy writer Russ Bravo came up with a funny sketch idea which explored the idea that the popular *Tellytubbies* appeared to be getting tubbier with every episode – Russ's mischievous suggestion was that this phenomenon was directly linked to a matching decline in the number of rabbits in each show.

Comedienne and writer Veronica McKenzie took the familiar format of TV commercials for floor cleaning products and developed it into a series of simple but very effective visual jokes as two cleaners made increasingly elaborate attempts to cross a puddle on a factory floor. The sketch's two heroines were accompanied at all times by the 'Mission Impossible' theme, proving that familiar sounds have just as much a part to play in sketch comedy as familiar images.

Jennifer Saunders, the creator of *Absolutely Fabulous*, and her comedy-writing partner Dawn French once told an interviewer that they got most of their sketch ideas from leafing through copies of society news magazine *Hello!* Whether or not they were being entirely serious, it's certainly true that, as with joke writing, it doesn't matter what triggers the ideas process so long as you actually end up with ideas. The best of those can then be refined into sketch material.

Once you've got your sketch idea, the next step is to put it into a suitable format for performance or broadcast. As a beginner you will either be producing your sketch comedy for production by yourself and whichever team of fellow writers and performers you are currently working with, or pitching your material to professional buyers. Even if you are producing sketches for yourself, in which case you don't strictly need a polished and professional looking script and can perform from notes on the back of an envelope if you so desire, you might still want to consider producing something laid out a bit more formally so that you end up with written examples of your best work for when you are pitching to other people.

138

If you are already targeting somebody else's show, whether that is a regular live sketch show or a broadcast format, make sure you analyse existing examples of these shows as thoroughly as possible. How long are the individual sketches in the existing show? Are there a number of short sketches or 'quickies' between the longer sketches? Do the sketches normally involve one, two or all of the featured actors in the show? Is there a member of the regular cast who is used less often than others? Is this because there aren't suitable sketches for his or her character? Are most of the sketches shot indoors or outdoors? Are there a lot of elaborate sets or costumes or are most of the sketches shot in 'reality' style?

Most of the sketch examples in this chapter are aimed at the broadcast market – whether traditional TV or the growing online market we will look at in more detail later – but if you are working on sketches for live performance or radio, the basic principle of studying the medium you are using and the resources available in terms of budget and cast numbers still applies.

Working out what is possible at an early stage will avoid lots of wasted work further down the line.

When the topical puppet show *Spitting Image* was on UK television in the 1990s and hungry for up-to-the minute material, quite a few sketches were commissioned from freelance writers and writers were even encouraged to send in work 'on spec'. Unfortunately, it appears that quite a few otherwise funny sketches which arrived from prospective writers had to be rejected because they called for physical actions such as running that the puppets weren't capable of in those pre-CGI days. A closer viewing of the show beforehand might have meant more of these sketches making it on to the air.

Quickies

Most novice writers will start their sketch-writing career by working on 'quickies'. Sometimes known as 'blackouts', these are very short sketches which, as the name suggests, usually involve one quick and often visual joke. In fact they are often visual versions of existing jokes. The one below is a good example:

Gambling quickie

Interior of Church. The **Minister** *is talking to a churchgoer.*

Churchgoer   You've got to help me, Reverend – I'm a sinner who has come to repent.

Minister   Praise the Lord! All you need to do is confess your sin and the Lord will show you the way . . .

Churchgoer   It's gambling – I just can't stop. Horse racing, poker, online casinos – I can't help myself . . .

Minister *takes out his Bible.*

Minister   Trust in the Lord, my son. For it says in the Twenty-Third Psalm: 'He is thy shepherd.' And in Corinthians Two: 'For when I am weak, You are strong,' and in Leviticus Nineteen, Verse One: 'Be holy because I the Lord am holy' . . .

Churchgoer   Don't stop, Reverend. You're really inspiring me!

Minister   Hallelujah! You've seen the error of your ways?

Churchgoer *takes out lottery ticket and pen.*

Churchgoer   No – but I only need one more number to be in with a chance of the jackpot!

In the music hall or vaudeville theatre there would traditionally have been a 'blackout' on the Minister's reaction to this gag. The whole stage would go dark and when the lights went back up there would be a new sketch or some other part of the show ready to begin. A quickie is like a single-panel cartoon – a comic snapshot with one joke – and there's nowhere to go with the characters after you have done the punchline.

Personally I have always believed that it is a good idea for writers pitching quickie and sketch material for the first time to have a punchline of some sort, even if your usual sense of humour is a bit more surreal. It's certainly true that many successful sketch shows such as *The League of Gentlemen* and the original *Monty Python* sketches don't necessarily end on a laugh. However, in cases like this the shows had already been commissioned, so producers were aware that there was no 'big laugh' at the end of the sketches because of artistic choice rather than because the writer couldn't manage one.

As a new writer sending in material 'cold' it is probably safer to have a good strong gag at the end of your sketch – just to show that you can. (But do make sure it's a good gag, not just one shoe-horned in to 'create' an ending.)

Although it was written for television the comedy sketch above could easily work on radio, with a few sound effects, maybe bells, organ music or the echoing sound of footsteps in church and one or two extra lines of dialogue (for instance, we'd have to be told about the Bible and the lottery ticket because we couldn't see them). The following sketch, however, has a purely visual punchline and wouldn't work on radio at all:

Bedtime quickie

Interior Bedroom. Close-up of **Mother** *leaning over child's bed (occupant out of shot)*

Mother You'll really have to stop being so nervous, darling. Mummy's just in the next room and I promise nothing scary is going to get you in the middle of the night. Now you go to sleep and I'll see you in the morning . . .

She leans over to tuck the 'child' in and we see that it's a thirty-year-old muscle-bound wrestler.

This is really just a visual version of the old joke about school which goes 'Of course you've got to go to school this morning darling – you're the headmaster', and would work just as well if a vampire, a ninja or any other 'fearless' adult was revealed in the final shot. Watch even a couple of TV sketch shows and you'll see that using the camera action to hold back visual information until the last minute is one of the most frequently used devices for creating quick laughs. It's called a 'pull back and reveal' sketch in the trade. Like all simple ideas, it can still work well, but the same rule applies here as to any trick of the comedy trade – use the same device too often and the audience will soon be able to predict that there is a surprise on the way.

The above sketch idea could be taken in a different direction on a darker show. Instead of the joke being that the 'child' is somebody who is big and scary themselves, the child could be an actual child expressing fears about the night, and the mother could start off by reassuring them as above, before starting to muse on all the things in the world which are really scary, from illness to rising crime rates to global warming, so that her attempts to comfort the child have the opposite effect.

In fact taking the sketch down this route could lead to a series of running sketches where the same character is seen as a telephone helpline operator, a hostage negotiator, a member of the cabin crew making a safety announcement – in each case she would start off saying calming things and slowly but surely escalate the examples of potential dangers she is giving to such a level that the people she is supposed to be calming are more terrified than they were when she first started.

Many regular sketch show characters have developed in this way and, instead of the joke being in not knowing what is going to happen as in the 'pull back and reveal' type of sketches, the laughter in character sketches comes from the regular audience knowing exactly where the sketch is going to go from the beginning.

We've already noted that practical cost factors are well worth taking into account when pitching sketches. In the example above, the bedroom would be a relatively easy scene to create in a studio. As it is a 'tight shot' you'd just need a bed, maybe with a cuddly toy or a cartoon-shaped lamp to suggest a child's room, and only two actors to play the mother and child. In our other variations, the helpline operator would just be one actor with a headset, the hostage negotiator might have a megaphone and be looking up towards an imaginary building under siege (we wouldn't necessarily need to show the building). Flashing light effects would enable us to show that it is a police scene without actually needing police vehicles. Obviously some of the shows you would be pitching to may have budgets which would actually allow police cars and extras to suggest a proper crime scene, but if your sketches work at basic level without needing a huge number of special props or casts of thousands there is a better chance of producers trying one out.

The importance of practicality is even more important when developing projects for the emerging online and new media markets. Sites like YouTube, Funny or Die and other online sources which enable writers and performers to upload their own comedy material are a huge leap forward in allowing people who want to break into the comedy field to do so directly without having to wait for the permission or funding of traditional production companies and networks. But precisely because you will be using these new platforms to bring your comedy material to the attention of the world, it is important to make sure that what you show is your best work.

Obviously you'll be aiming to produce scripts which are just as professional and high quality as if you were working for commercial clients, but it is also important to take into account the practical aspects of the medium you are working in. For instance, many video sharing sites currently have a limit to the number of minutes' worth of material you can upload at one time. Although this limit is expanding as internet speeds get faster and faster, it makes sense to be aware of how long a sketch can run at maximum length (and also to bear in mind that almost every comedy piece benefits by being shorter rather than longer).

Bear in mind also that people will watch your finished work on a wide variety of different types of screen with very varied picture quality and size of image. Your own budget will also dictate what quality of sound and picture is possible for your work. With this in mind, you may want to check if the sketch ideas you have are big and broad enough to come across clearly even when watched on small screens, in exactly the same way that a sketch which might work well in an intimate comedy venue may not communicate as well to a large stadium audience.

Just as a producer would do on a low-budget TV comedy show, you need to think clearly about the minimum number of visual elements you can use to 'suggest' locations where your online comedy is taking place as opposed to setting it in big or detailed locations which, even if you can afford to visit them or build them, may not come across clearly to the viewer watching the sketch on a smaller or less sharp computer or phone screen.

For similar cost and camera availability reasons, many sketches and quickies on both stage and screen feature just two performers – hence the name 'two-handers'. Comedy double acts have always needed two-hander type material, of course, but just as putting two topics together in a brainstorm can usually lead to a joke of some sort, putting two characters together in any given situation is usually a good way to create a sketch, as long as both characters have different motivations from each other. Although improvisational comics sometimes extract humour from going in the opposite direction and having two diverse characters agree with each other to such an exaggerated level that it becomes funny, the usual sketch participants tend to be two characters who are in conflict in some way or other. As an example, this two-hander was written for a show broadcasting at a time when police attitudes to ethnic minorities were attracting controversy and in particular when drives to attract ethnic minority officers to join the police force were being denounced by minority communities as a smokescreen to hide the fact that harassment was still ongoing.

Police Two-Hander

Interior living room. An older black woman is laying the table for dinner. We hear loud, aggressive knocking on the door.

Police woman *(off camera)*   Open up! I know you're in there! Don't make me have to break this door down.

Old Woman *angrily opens the door.* Black **Policewoman** *enters.*

Old Woman   Go on, then – beat me up! That's right – cuff me and take me down to the station.

Police woman   I'm not here to arrest you. I just want to ask you a question.

Old Woman   That's what you all say – nothing to do but come round harassing innocent people.

Policewoman   That's not what I'm here for at all.

Policewoman *reaches out her hand to calm the woman.*

Old Woman   Don't you touch me – you're worse than any of them. Wearing that uniform and selling out your own community.

Policewoman   Look, all I want to do is ask you one question. Why don't you just make it easy on both of us?

Old Woman   OK, I give up. Ask your question . . .

Policewoman *sits down at the table, and* **Old Woman** *throws a plate of food in front of her.*

Policewoman   It's the same question as always, Mum – why do we have to go through this every night when I come home for my dinner?

Even though the above sketch is longer and more involved than our previous examples, and centres on what was then (and sadly still is) a hot topic, it still comes across as more of a quickie than a character-based sketch because there really isn't much that is funny about it (at least from the writing point of view) until the punchline. The end of the sketch is very much in 'pull back and reveal' style but twisted so that instead of holding back some visual information to 'fill in the blanks' at the end, we used the very visual clue of the policewoman's uniform to distract from the fact that she was also the older woman's daughter until it was time for the reveal.

We're also in quickie territory because it's highly unlikely that the older woman would forget that her daughter was a police officer or behave in this very exaggerated way every time she came home. You could probably find a way to develop the two characters into other sketches – after all, there are lots of tensions between parents and children around career and life choices – but the humour would need to be based on the tension between the two women rather than the surprise of their being related, as this has already been revealed.

As with all the other rules and advice given in these pages, this is as good a time as any to remind you that rules are made to be broken. Having told you earlier that just stringing a series of jokes together isn't usually the best way to produce a good sketch, here is an extract from a sketch written by Russ Bravo which does just that. As a deliberate homage to the very traditional music hall type of double-act sketch, with a touch of the famous Parrot Sketch thrown in, you will see that Russ has obviously done a great deal of brainstorming to generate pet shop related jokes and puns, the more excruciating the better:

Pet Shop Sketch
Interior Pet Shop. The **Owner** *is behind the counter as the* **Comedian** *enters.*

Comedian   Have you got any Koi Carp?

Owner   No, but I could do you an embarrassed hamster.

Comedian   Fine, I'll take a dozen – I need to re-stuff my duvet.

Owner   You can't use hamsters for that . . .

Comedian   Why? Do you think gerbils would be better?

Owner   I'll get the Animal Protection people on to you, mate.

Comedian   Hey, I didn't know they did a duvet-stuffing service!

Owner   Look, for your duvet you want duck down.

Comedian *ducks down*

Comedian   What? Like this?

Owner   No – duck down from ducks. Or goose feathers.

Comedian   Goose feathers? No way – they were dead uncomfortable last time.

Owner   Why?

Comedian   They still had the goose attached.

. . . and so on through the entire animal kingdom. You may wish to amuse yourself (or drive yourself mad!) by continuing the dialogue and coming up with a suitable ending. While this type of sketch is a tribute to the very traditional straight man/funny man type of double act, in that the store owner has no jokes and is there to feed straight lines to the comic, many modern comedy duos don't have as clear a distinction between the two performers. And of course there are just as many funny women in the business as there are funny men. The sketch by writer Sharon Otway below is written for two actresses but centres on a problem that both sexes can relate to – going to buy food when you are already hungry.

Hungry
Exterior. Shopping Mall. Daytime

Debbie *and* **Dawn** *are on their lunch break.*

Debbie   OK – let's get lunch from the supermarket. I'm starving.

Dawn   Lunch? We've only got £2.50 – you'd better swallow your pride and go to the cheap cafe.

Debbie   Come on, I'm not going to buy the whole shop, just some small treats. I always feel good after I've shopped.

Cut to:

Interior. Supermarket.
Dawn *and* **Debbie** *are at the checkout with a huge mountain of food, drink, etc.*

Debbie   I told you we should have got a basket.

Dawn *just looks on in horror.*

Cashier   That'll be £275.65, please.

Debbie   But we've only got £2.50.

Cashier   I think you'd be better off going to that cheap cafe.

Besides exaggerating a situation that most of us have got into at one time or other, the appeal of this sketch is visual – an impossibly large mountain of food. The main appeal of visual comedy sketches to the working comedy writer and to production companies is that they work equally well in different languages. As our world becomes increasingly connected, a major source of revenue for broadcasters is the sale of home-produced material to overseas markets either in its original form or as a 'format' that can be remade locally with actors from whatever country the show has been sold to. Styles and fashions in comedy differ from country to country, and some of the more traditional types of comedy, such as slapstick, which are not so much in vogue in Britain or America are still popular in other territories. We'll be looking at marketing via the internet in our next chapter, but even in pre-internet days it was not unusual for British-based comedy writers to derive a lot of their income from selling work to European networks who tend to make more sketch and variety based shows than producers in the UK. Not only is writing for foreign markets a possible source of extra income and exposure, it is also a very good way to find out how much of your comedy is language based – and to discover how difficult it is to get jokes which rely on the quirks and anomalies of the English language to work well in other tongues.

As with all the sketches we have used as examples so far, it goes without saying that much of the success of the food sketch would rely on the skill of the actresses playing Debbie and Dawn to create the right note of frustration and embarrassment. One of the delights of working on sketch scripts is watching the final performance and seeing how a good cast can get laughs from lines – or even just from glances – that you hadn't expected. But it cuts both ways: even the most accomplished performers can do little without a script to base their performance on.

True-life stories

The best sketches, like the best stand-up routines, are usually the ones which have been developed from believable situations that everybody in the audience can connect with, which are funny all the way through and which end on a strong punchline. Like all good comedy, this winning combination can only be achieved through a process of trial, error and experimentation.

The following sketch was written for the pilot of a sketch show called *Comedy Republic* by talented stand-up comic and writer Karola Gajda. As an example of good solid comedy sketch writing it would be likely to attract attention from any kind of sketch show. It's a clever but simple idea, combining humour all the way through with a good solid joke at the end. And just as importantly it didn't cost the earth to shoot. Karola tells me that the inspiration for the sketch came out of anger – 'I got really annoyed about a friend of mine who was constantly being sent to interview for unsuitable jobs just so she could continue being eligible for social security payments, and I thought wouldn't it be funny to deliberately mess up the interviews?' Combining that thought with the observation that many people bring stuffed animals and other 'lucky mascots' with them to interviews and exams produced the results below:

Interview Sketch

Interior. Waiting Area. Day.

We see a candidate leaving an office, and hear the manager's voice (off camera) saying 'Thanks for coming in – we'll be contacting successful candidates next week'. Our man is waiting outside and is ushered in.

Cut to:

Interior. Office. **Man** *is sitting down at desk with* **Interviewer** *on other side.*

Interviewer   Hello, Mr Jones.

Man   Hello, Miss Booth.

Interviewer   Well, we have your details here from the job centre – quite impressive. So what made you apply for the position of bank clerk?

Man   Excuse me, do you mind awfully . . .

Man takes a cuddly rabbit out of his bag and puts it on the desk.

Man   It's my lucky mascot, Thumper. My deceased mother gave it to me as a child and I have to have him with me wherever I go. Sorry if it seems a bit weird . . . I'm just a bit nervous.

Interviewer   Oh . . .

(She is obviously surprised but makes an effort to continue normally)

That's OK . . . it's quite sweet really . . . we all have our quirky superstitions, don't we?

Man *(offended)*   Oh, this isn't superstition – this is fact.

(To rabbit.)

Isn't it, Thumper?

Interviewer is looking increasingly concerned but still keeping up a front.

Interviewer   Anyway, where were we? What skills do you—

Man   Would you have a saucer of water, please? Thumper says he's rather thirsty – he's feeling nervous as well, you see.

Interviewer   I really don't think this is quite normal. Is this some kind of joke?

Man   Do you mind if I give him a carrot? He normally has his eleven o'clock snack around now.

Interviewer Really, Mr Jones, this sort of behaviour isn't helping you one bit. I don't see any point in carrying on this interview.

Man begins to thump rabbit viciously.

Man You've done it again. You've done it again. I've had enough of you. I've lost my chance again. It's all your fault.

Cut to:

Man being pushed out of the office door, which slams after him.

Man *(joyfully)* Great! One more boring job I won't get!

He takes out his welfare cheque and waves it triumphantly.

Man Hurrah! I love you, social security!

He gives Thumper a big kiss.

Ends

The interviewee in Karola's sketch was played by very expressive actor and comedian Logan Murray, and as well as the basic joke idea it was the interaction between Logan and the interviewer's rising unease, as well as his conversations with the bunny rabbit, which made the sketch work. You'll note that as the way lines were delivered in this sketch was crucial Karola included some directions in her script for clarity but still left lots of room for the actors to bring their characters to life.

It is this same combination of character-based comedy and the ability to ask 'What if?' questions that best equips a writer to shine on the next rung of the comedy ladder . . .

Sitcom writing

For many comedy writers, the creation of a long-running and successful sitcom is the ultimate 'Holy Grail'. Not only is this perceived as one of the most highly paid areas of television writing, but there is also the satisfaction of knowing that millions of viewers are tuning into your show week after week to laugh at characters and situations you have created.

Of course in the modern era, the 'facts' behind the above picture of sitcom success are a little different both from the heyday of huge sitcom hits like *Friends* or *Frasier* and from the reality for most modern sitcom writers. With the advent of user controlled TV, it is much less likely that the nation will sit down to watch even the top sitcoms at the same time, or every week. Some people will watch the show on its first airing while others will watch reruns night after night as today's TV schedulers often prefer to schedule in nightly 'blocks' rather than on a programme-by-programme basis (and these days shows can often start to rerun as soon as their original airing is over). Other viewers may watch the show in an online or digital format while on the move and there are also people who prefer to wait for the series boxed set to come out on DVD and watch all the episodes in one sitting.

All of the above exposure depends on the show being successful in the first place, of course, and it is usually at this point that the high earning potential of sitcom writing kicks in – assuming that you or your agent have negotiated your repeat fees and usage rights properly.

For the working comedy writer, getting to this stage will usually involve working either as an individual or more likely as part of a team on many low-budget pilot projects, some of which will be aired very quietly on smaller cable channels and some which may never get beyond the live run-through or initial pilot recording.

If this sounds negative, it isn't meant to. In actual fact many of the 'classic' BBC sitcoms such as *Blackadder* and *Dad's Army* started off as try-outs, not getting hugely favourable reviews when originally aired, and have only reached their current iconic status through perseverance and ongoing development. *Seinfeld* is a US-based example of a sitcom which is now considered a milestone but when first aired (as *The Seinfeld Chronicles*) barely made it past pilot stage due to an initially poor response from the network.

Starting in a low-budget way certainly doesn't mean a show cannot become hugely successful – however, it is important to note that the 'turnaround' for all of the above shows came when particular TV executives believed in them strongly enough to champion them through their early rocky development period. The modern TV market is less forgiving, with the result that shows need to become hits much faster or they may be dropped. The good news is that as so many shows don't make it, it does mean that there is always going to be a market for new ideas and for writers who can turn those new ideas into viable series. However, the reality is that today's writers also need the discipline and commitment to work on each new project like it is going to be the next sitcom classic, even if they are fully aware that the last ten or twenty projects they may have worked equally hard on didn't make the final cut.

Certainly, the difficulty of succeeding in this area doesn't stop TV producers and networks being bombarded by new sitcom ideas and scripts every year from both professional and amateur writers. As with other forms of comedy writing, making your work stand out from this avalanche will involve carefully researching exactly what makes sitcom different from other kinds of comedy before you start writing, and also studying the types of sitcom which are currently being commissioned rather than just your old favourites before you start pitching (bearing in mind that in today's ever-changing media world 'old' can mean last season's hit shows!).

Broadly speaking there are two routes into sitcom writing – the first, which has been more usually the case in the UK market, is for a single writer or a writing team to develop an original sitcom idea and pitch it to a production company who will in turn pitch it to one of the networks. The second, which has been the norm in America for many years (and is increasingly becoming the model favoured in Britain too), is to have sitcoms written by teams, so that the aspiring writer's first sample script won't be based on their own characters and concept but instead a demonstration that they can write a usable script for whichever existing sitcom they are hoping to join.

In terms of either avenue, the key to success isn't just knowing what to do to write good situation comedy but also being aware of the common mistakes which lose many writers their chance even before the potential producer has read the first scene.

Sitcom concepts

Probably the single biggest mistake beginners make is to take the term 'situation comedy' at face value. If you study any good sitcom over several episodes you will see that very little of the humour arises directly from situations. In fact sitcom plots are often quite mundane – a missed wedding anniversary, having to cover up a lie or, as in a classic *Hancock's Half Hour*, a single character confined to their own home for an entire episode with nothing to do and nobody to talk to but themselves. It is well worth tracking down and watching that particular show, 'The Bedsitter', to see what talented writers Galton and Simpson can do with such a thin premise. Perhaps as a direct result many other sitcoms since Hancock have featured similar episodes, with the main character or just one or two of the regular cast confined to some small space with nothing to produce comedy from but their own interactions. Watch a variety of old and new sitcoms even over a short period of time and you will quickly notice a relatively small number of recurring plot situations and set-ups popping up over and over again.

What makes these situations interesting, no matter how mundane they are, or how many times we have seen similar plots before, is the way the individual characters in the show respond and react to them.

Think about the chaos John Cleese as Basil Fawlty would inevitably create trying to compensate for a missed wedding anniversary – he'd certainly never admit to having missed it, and his attempts to fix the situation would probably be driven more by fear of his wife Sybil's wrath than by any sense of affection. Meanwhile Homer Simpson truly loves his wife, Marge, but probably forgets their wedding anniversary every year. He might try to pretend that he is planning a surprise for her – which will no doubt end in disaster – or he might admit that he has forgotten and be so ashamed that he runs away from home (and almost certainly into some new disaster). In the case of the Simpsons, solving the problem will usually involve other regular characters and members of the family, while the Basil Fawlty character's gift for turning even the smallest drama into a crisis is based on the fact that he rarely listens to any advice but his own.

I'm not suggesting for a moment that strong plots and clever twists to situations are unimportant in sitcom writing, but in order to get the best out of our plots and situations, our first task as sitcom writers is to come up with a cast of interesting characters that our viewers will want to return to and spend time with episode after episode.

Note that I said 'interesting' characters – not necessarily overtly funny ones. Certainly characters like Basil Fawlty and Homer Simpson are larger-than-life creations (literally so when it comes to Homer's waistline!) but they need slightly more normal characters surrounding them to act as a contrast to their craziness, whether it is Polly, the sensible maid at Fawlty Towers, or Lisa, Homer's studious, politically aware daughter (who must frequently wonder if she has been adopted).

There are also very successful sitcoms where the central characters are the relatively normal ones and it is the characters that surround them who are more 'extreme'. In the popular British sitcom *The Good Life*, Tom and Barbara Good, as played by Richard Briers and Felicity Kendal, were an ordinary middle class couple who had decided to live in an eco-friendly way and grow organic food (a very radical lifechange for the 1970s). Much of the comedy in the show came from the contrast between their attempts to live a more simple life and Penelope Keith's characterisation of highly aspirational and upwardly mobile neighbour Margo whose mission in life was to do exactly the opposite.

In the US sitcom *Scrubs*, the central character JD is relatively normal compared to more extreme characters like the sexually obsessed Todd and the very disturbing Janitor (although, as in many long-running sitcoms, by the end of *Scrubs* even the more cartoonish regular characters became more human and rounded). Famously, *Seinfeld* was a 'comedy where nothing happens'. In the title role, stand-up comedian Jerry Seinfeld's task was often to make observations on and try to restore order to the extreme behaviour of the other regular characters.

What every sitcom needs is a cast of contrasting personalities – some may be 'normal', some may be exaggerated. Some may be knowingly funny and deliberately sarcastic, others may do and say things which are funny but in an entirely unintentional way. However you set up your own regular cast, the more differences and contrasts between them, the more story ideas will result and the funnier your telling of those stories will be.

Sitcom themes

Just as there are standard sitcom characters, the same sitcom themes recur again and again. Probably the two most common types of sitcom setting are, firstly, family-based shows – be they happy families (*The Cosby Show*, *Modern Family*), squabbling families (*Till Death Us Do Part*, *All in the Family*) or 'non-traditional' family units (*The Munsters*, *Will & Grace*, *Two and a Half Men*) and secondly, workplace-based shows like *Taxi*, *Scrubs* or *30 Rock*.

Having already noted that it is contrasts and conflicts between diverse characters that generate sitcom laughter, it should be obvious why family and work themes have proven so popular with show creators. Not only does each type of setting bring a very contrasting cast of characters together in a relatively confined setting – whether this is the family home or the shared workplace – it is precisely because of family ties or the need to make a living that characters who wouldn't normally choose to interact regularly with each other are forced to do so over and over again.

This element is important in sitcom creation not just from a comedy point of view but also a practical one. Most sitcoms, especially in the early stages, don't have the budget for more than a small number of regular sets, so it is important that the characters can believably play out their stories in these same locations. Home and workplaces fit the bill perfectly because they are places we all visit regularly. It is only when sitcoms like *Friends* become successful that the budget expands to allow trips to overseas locations for special episodes.

There are of course sitcom themes which interpret the 'trap diverse characters together' principle in more creative and exaggerated ways. Back in the 1960s one of America's best remembered sitcoms, *Gilligan's Island*, literally marooned its characters on an island, as did one of the 1990s' most successful UK sitcoms, *Father Ted*. The BBC's science fiction comedy *Red Dwarf* went one further and trapped its cast in a spaceship on the outer reaches of the galaxy.

It is worth noting, however, that even in the shows which are set in the 'exciting' worlds of media, medicine or outer space, the comedy still arises from the petty squabbles and jealousies which affect human life in more 'ordinary' environments.

Creating a hit concept

As with all television ideas, a sitcom concept must perform the seemingly impossible balancing act of being fresh and new enough to attract viewer interest and ratings, while at the same time being familiar and 'proven' enough to give the producers the confidence to commit the time and resources necessary to make the show in the first place.

It's not surprising, therefore, that successful sitcom concepts throughout the history of the medium have often featured very similar themes. The 1970s saw popular medical-based sitcoms on both sides of the Atlantic. Both the UK's *Doctor in the House* and the USA series *M*A*S*H* were spin-offs from popular movies. By the 1980s and 1990s medical sitcoms were still popular but with a 'twist'. In the case of the UK's *Surgical Spirit* the twist – radical for the time – was that the central character was a female surgeon, while the American series *Doogie Howser MD* featured a sixteen-year-old child prodigy who wrestled with the contradictions of being a fully-fledged doctor while still being a normal teenager. Medical-based comedy continued to be very much alive and well in the twenty-first century, with the very dark comedy of the UK's *Green Wing* and the USA's long-running ensemble series *Scrubs* proudly flying the flag. No doubt there will be further forays into the medical field by British and American writers as the century progresses.

Although all these series had a common medical theme, each one had its own unique brand of humour and cast of characters, and each had very specific elements reflecting the tastes of its own era. This is equally true of the many sitcoms which have taken the world of media as their theme. In the 1970s *The Mary Tyler Moore Show* was set in a busy newsroom where despite all the banter and minor relationship conflicts, the news team were basically a warm, friendly family unit. In later media-set sitcoms such as *Drop the Dead Donkey*, *The Larry Sanders Show* or *30 Rock* the humour has become a lot less warm and often extremely cynical.

What both the medical field and the media world have in common, and perhaps the reason why they are so popular with sitcom writers, is that they are both worlds which allow scope for a range of diverse characters, where insecurities and power struggles abound and where viewers enjoy discovering that despite the supposed glamour or importance of the job, the people who do it are as fallible and awkward as the rest of us.

Memorable and larger than life central characters also contribute to the uniqueness of a hit show – but again, it is often the spark of humanity behind the exaggerated outer shell which keeps us coming back to engage with them. As played by Jennifer Saunders, Edina, the central character of *Absolutely Fabulous*, may be the epitome of spaced-out, new age, self-help obsessive, but we can see that she secretly wants the love and respect of her daughter and co-workers and that is what warms us to her. Homer Simpson may be a walking disaster as a father, but there is something lovable about his underlying devotion to his family and the sincere repentance that usually follows each failure.

By all means strive to be new and contemporary in your own sitcom creations, but be aware that something new can become something old very quickly. When breakfast television was first introduced in Britain, there were many sitcom proposals doing the rounds about what goes on behind the scenes, but perhaps because of this overkill, none of them ever made it to series, and if they had, they might look very dated now that breakfast TV is as much 'part of the furniture' as every other kind of TV. Cybercafes and video rental outlets are other settings which might once have been cutting edge but have now been superseded by advances in technology. Of course, you might decide to deliberately choose a bygone era and thereby render your concept 'timeless': wartime sitcom *Dad's Army*, the 1950s-based *Happy Days* and *That '70s Show* remain perennial favourites in the rerun schedules. As a first-time writer though, remember that heavily costume and prop-based shows may be easier to sell when producers have seen your worth with less expensive and complicated first projects.

Whatever concept you decide on, a new idea or a new variation on an old theme will stand or fall on whether you have a strong enough cast of regular characters to derive as much comedy as possible from their circumstances.

Now let's look at some ways of generating plot ideas to help them do just that.

Sitcom plots

Perhaps you are a new writer aiming to break into sitcom writing by joining an already established team on a current show (as is usually the route in America and increasingly the route in Britain). Or you may be developing your own sitcom either from scratch or perhaps because you have been commissioned to do so to fill a particular time slot. Either way if you have good, strong characters to work with it should be possible to create good comedy from their responses to any given plot or situation. This doesn't mean that you should be lazy about plot development and simply recycle the same stories over and over again. Like classic jokes, some of the best sitcom plots are so well known that the only way to use them these days is in a deliberately ironic way. However, if, as often happens in today's media world, you are faced with having to turn out a lot of half-hour scripts in a very short space of time, or that one brilliant sample script, it is reassuring to know that your main task *isn't* to come up with the world's funniest and most original plot – it's to come up with basic, well-structured plots and then find funny, original ways for your cast of characters to act them out.

If you are submitting a sample script based on an existing sitcom and on somebody else's characters, it is obviously vital that you take the time to study the concept and characters so thoroughly that your script feels like a regular script from the series. But even if you are working on an original idea, make sure you know your own characters well enough that they remain consistent all the way through. Remember the producers are looking not just for 'one good episode' or even 'one good series' but for the potential to generate enough stories to carry you and them through as many successful seasons as possible.

Often the quickest way to establish if your characters work or not is to use the bare bones of an existing plot from movies, TV shows (not necessarily comedies), literature or fairy tales or simply from something that happened to you or somebody you know. If your characters are strong enough they should play out the story in a funny, original way that, although it may follow the same basic map as the original, ends up being a very different end product.

If you are basing your sample script on existing characters, or if you are aiming to brainstorm a number of different storylines to show that your own original characters have long-running potential, it can be very useful to ask 'What if?' questions.

What if Frasier were to be hypnotised? What if Joey from *Friends* became US President? Once you have the basic question, your task is to explore the storyline in a way which is funny but also consistent with the characters as they behave in other episodes of the show. I have of course used those two well-known characters from classic sitcoms no longer in production for illustration purposes only. If you are pitching to join an existing show you would of course be asking 'What if?' questions about the characters from that show or, if doing a sample script, basing it on a *current* sitcom.

That said, let's tease out the Frasier illustration further – why would Dr Crane want to be hypnotised? Maybe he has a crisis of confidence and needs to relax – but given that the character is a psychiatrist, would he really believe in, let alone submit to, hypnosis, at least as a first resort? OK, so maybe he meets a stage hypnotist via his radio show or at a convention and only agrees to be hypnotised to 'prove' that non-medical hypnosis is a sham. But of course it does work . . . However, to make the story funnier let's arrange things so that it looks at first like it hasn't worked. Little does the triumphant Frasier know that the hypnotist has left him with a 'trigger' word that will cause him to fall asleep.

You'll note that there are no right or wrong answers to this exploring process, only answers that move the story forward and are consistent with the feel of the show. Give a basic situation like this to ten comedy writers and each one will develop it in an entirely different way. But whatever plots you do come up with there are a few special sitcom 'rules' to keep in mind.

The first, especially for new or sample scripts, is that plots should make as much use as possible of the regular cast. Be wary of plots which rely too much on outside characters to drive the story. There are two reasons for this: firstly, if you have created a strong enough cast, the comedy should naturally arise from their interaction, and if you are working with existing characters the producer will want to see how well you work with those characters rather than new characters of your own. Secondly, your producer won't be too keen on paying an expensive cast of regular actors just to have them stand around doing nothing while you give all the best lines to even more expensive guest stars.

With that in mind, maybe we should remove the 'hypnotist' character from our Frasier plot and instead have Frasier accidentally hypnotised by his brother Niles when the two psychiatric siblings have a professional disagreement about whether or not the treatment works.

As often happened in the actual *Frasier* series, one or two of the lead characters may be the prime drivers of each episode's plot, but make sure the other regulars also get a look-in. Usually the subplot in a sitcom episode not only involves the rest of the regular cast (or certainly the ones who are less involved in the lead story) but also echoes or relates to the main plot in some way.

As well as being driven by the regular characters, sitcom plots should make good use of the regular sets. It is always a good idea to think of the three or four locations which offer the most versatility when creating your own shows, as you are likely to be using them quite often.

You can, of course, have freer rein with guest celebrities and outside locations when your show takes off, but at the early stages it is best to use creativity rather than money when telling stories that involve a lot of travel. Even in *Taxi*, a sitcom which was for obvious reasons very travel based, the bulk of the storylines were played out in the depot where the cabs parked and the drivers waited for their next fare.

While budgets are as much if not more of a concern for sitcom producers as they ever were, other 'hard and fast' rules of the genre have become a bit more flexible with each new generation. It used to be an unbreakable rule that no matter what disaster was threatened at the beginning of a sitcom episode, no matter which characters had a falling-out and no matter how likely it looked that the bar would close, the castaways would be rescued or something else would happen to destroy the premise of the show, the status quo would always be restored at the end of each episode. While some shows continue this tradition, shows like *Friends* have taken sitcom into more fluid territory with plotlines which continue and develop from episode to episode and series to series. Shows like *Curb Your Enthusiasm*, which feature a lot of improvisation from the actors in addition to scripted dialogue and plot, have further blurred the line between 'messy' reality and the slick sitcom world of the past where every plot was neatly tied up in 25–30 minutes.

In encouraging you to keep up to date with the styles and approaches to sitcom which are most popular in the current market, it is still worth bearing in mind that when you are pitching new projects as an unknown writer it can be useful to take the approach recommended to jazz singers referred to earlier – you will be given more chances to improvise and take your music in new directions if you first prove you can play the notes in the right order.

The problem

Perhaps because so many basic sitcom concepts and characters don't change from episode to episode, one commonly used technique to generate involving stories is to create a problem that needs to be solved. The problem may be trivial or serious depending on the theme and flavour of the individual sitcom, but it must be enough of a problem that we will want to stay with the show to see how the characters solve it – or to see what will happen to them if they don't.

The problem is often a very good thing to introduce as we develop our 'What if?' ideas. After all, if the answer to 'What would happen if . . .' is 'Not very much' there wouldn't be much reason to stay around to watch the episode.

So let's see if we can develop the 'Frasier is hypnotised' idea a bit further by throwing in a problem. We decided that while Frasier thinks the hypnosis experiment has had no effect on him, the hypnotist has (probably accidentally) instilled a trigger word into his subconscious which will make him fall asleep the moment he hears it. Maybe the trigger word is 'crane' – a word which he is going to hear very often as it is his surname – or it may be 'Seattle', which would also be quite likely to pop up a lot in conversation because he lives there. Whatever the word we choose we would then try to put him into some situation – perhaps speaking at a conference or making the pilot for a TV version of his radio show which he has been working hard on pitching for months on end – where it would be a very big problem if he kept falling asleep every time somebody mentioned his name or his home city.

We can get a lot of comedy as he tries to cover up the fact that he keeps dozing off, and perhaps develop the plot by having him slowly discover which word is causing the problem so that he begins to find all sorts of creative ways to avoid hearing it or prevent other people from saying it (after all, he is still not going to give the stage hypnotist the satisfaction of knowing his experiment actually works). Just when he thinks he has that problem under control, we introduce a bigger one – his producer announces that the cable channel he has made the pilot for loves the show, and will put it on nightly, thanks to the sponsor she has found – The Seattle Crane Company. It looks like Frasier will be hearing the dreaded words a lot more often.

Will he continue to try to disguise his sleepy condition? Will he have to swallow his pride and get his adversary to unhypnotise him? Will the hypnotist be able to do so, because he doesn't know how he did it in the first place? These are the questions that will hopefully keep the viewers watching till the end of the show.

As an exercise you may want to have a go at fleshing out this rough plotline using either the Frasier characters, the cast of your own favourite sitcom past or present or characters of your own. Whatever direction you take with the plot, remember that the outcome can't be that Frasier actually becomes a TV presenter or stays hypnotised. As in most sitcoms, for better or worse, we need to tell a story worth telling but for the practical reasons already given (unless we are the head writer or executive producer with the power to make major format changes) we need to tell it in a way that ends up back with the status quo.

Sitcom structure

Once your sitcom structure has been worked out, at last you can put it into script form. To get an idea of standard sitcom structures, and especially to get a feel for the variety of sitcom structures currently in vogue, watch as many of the latest series as you can. Don't just pay attention to the dialogue, plot and performance (although these are important) but keep an eye also on length of scenes, and even how many individual shots are in each scene. Are they long shots, mid shots or reaction shots? Ultimately it will be the director who decides on these last points but being aware of how your work may be filmed will help you keep a suitable rhythm in mind when you are writing your scripts.

Most 'half-hour' sitcoms last somewhere between 24 and 28 minutes depending on commercial breaks and/or presentation links and station identification promos. If there are breaks in the show, the individual segments may or may not be of equal length and if you are watching a show in rerun, or one which has been imported from a different country, be aware that scenes may have been edited out. (These days this is much less likely to be related to censorship and is usually more to do with fitting the show into a particular scheduling gap.)

At the beginning just try to keep your finished script to somewhere around the 25-minute mark – even if it is eventually commissioned it will go through a lot of drafting and redrafting before it actually hits the screen.

What you do need to ensure is that your story, like all pieces of drama, conforms to a basic 'three-act structure'. There are many good general books on dramatic writing which will explain this structure in detail but essentially it means that every plot should have a beginning, middle and end. The three acts do not need to be of equal length – usually the third act is the shortest as it is the one that wraps up the story, but the number of scenes in each act will vary depending on the style of the show you are working on. As you may have seen from your own research, shows which are filmed in front of a live audience may have between eight and twenty separate scenes. The majority of studio-based US shows tend to centre their action in the studio with very fleeting outside scenes, while British studio-based shows often have quite lengthy scenes filmed on location and juxtaposed with the studio-based stuff. Increasingly both countries are now producing shows which are filmed rather than taped in front of an audience with the result that there is more scope to move around. Most modern shows which are not filmed live no longer use 'canned laughter' to stand in for the live audience sound – and most comedy fans feel this is a good thing.

For a very clever demonstration of the difference between the modern style of sitcom and the more traditional 'studio audience' show, track down a copy of the *Scrubs* episode entitled 'My life in three cameras' where the lead character JD fantasises about what his life would be like if it were an old-style sitcom. The contrast between the multi-camera, highly glossy and brightly lit *Scrubs* in the fantasy version and the 'real world' of the show's regular and grittier single camera look is stark indeed.

Below I have listed some of the most common elements of a typical sitcom episode. Not all of them feature in every current sitcom and, as already noted, some are designed to be edited out if necessary depending on which network they are being shown on, but it is useful to keep them in mind as you break down your own stories.

Teaser

As its name implies, this is a short comic sequence often lasting no more than a minute, which takes place either before the title sequence or, in some sitcoms, while the opening credits are rolling. Sometimes it has a direct relation to the plot that is about to unfold, and sometimes it's just a snappy little piece of comedy designed to catch the viewer's attention.

Act One

This is where we set up the plot of the episode. For instance, a perennial situation is the one where somebody very important is coming to dinner and everything must be perfect. In the fifties and sixties it could well have been the boss who might give the husband a promotion so the pressure was on his wife to prepare a flawless meal. (Of course if the wife in question happened to be Lucille Ball that was unlikely to happen.)

In more recent times it might be a record producer wanting to discuss a lucrative deal or maybe neighbours from a different religious or ethnic group who our lead characters do not want to offend. In this act we also introduce the problem: let's say an obnoxious brother-in-law, aunt or family friend who turns up unannounced just as the Important Guest is sitting down to eat.

Act Two

The plot thickens. Usually in sitcom terms this means that the worst possible thing happens. Not only does the obnoxious aunt arrive at the same time as the boss but she is very drunk. Luckily she is also incoherent, so our hero makes increasingly frantic and imaginative attempts to 'translate' each muttered insult, obscenity or racial slur back to the boss as something complimentary. How well or how badly he achieves this will depend on the personality we gave him when we created our lead character – if you are pitching to an existing show this is the kind of scene where you can demonstrate that you know the characters. How our lead handles this must not only be funny but also how the regular audience and writers would expect him to handle it based on his established personality traits.

At the point where our hero seems to be getting away with his plan to save the evening, we introduce something even worse than the worst thing that has already happened: Auntie starts to sober up. Not enough to become any friendlier but more than enough to be clearly understood. Just as she is about to say something really over the top, along comes our commercial break if we have one. By now our viewers should be hooked enough to stay with the channel until they find out what happens.

Act Three

We're back after the break, and just as Auntie is about to unleash the killer insult . . . a new party guest arrives and further distracts her. This guest is likely to be a member of our regular cast that we may not have seen much in this episode and his or her visit may be related to whatever subplot has been going on in the episode. Although it looks like we have been reprieved, the new guest actually makes matters worse by offering Auntie more drink and getting her involved in conversation about scandalous things she did back in her schooldays. (We would probably have established earlier that the boss has a reputation for being prudish.) As always, we're trying to make the situation worse and worse so we can make our lead character's responses more and more extreme.

Climax

This is usually the point in the show where it looks like our main character's world is about to fall apart. Surely the boss will not only withhold the raise/record deal/promotion or whatever other prize he is here to bestow but quite probably fire our hero for letting this dinner fiasco happen.

But then we learn that the boss is sick of everyone always being false when they meet him and he loved Auntie's earthiness and honesty. Or maybe he too had a drink problem earlier in his life and so he knows what the pressure can be like. Or maybe he only just recognised that Auntie was the girl who he had a crush on all through school but she was too stuck-up to give him the time of day. Or . . . it doesn't matter whether you go with one of these suggestions or come up with a better one of your own. What *does* matter is that the journey to this point has been a funny one and that however we resolve the problem it is believable and satisfying and doesn't change the basic premise of the show too much.

Epilogue or tag

This short sequence (sometimes played out over the closing credits) may or may not relate back to the episode plot. It might also involve the tying up of the subplot. Often it is just a subtle piece of character interaction that makes us smile and leaves us wanting to come back for more in the next episode.

To be continued . . . ?

One reason why it is hard to give a standard format or structure for sitcom scripts is that the genre is constantly changing and developing, both in terms of content and in terms of production methods. Shows like *The Young Ones* or *Soap*, which were once considered 'edgy' and the 'next big thing', are still fun to watch but now have the cosy glow of nostalgia about them. No doubt with the passing of time this will happen even to the newest and most 'out there' shows of today. If sitcom is one of your career goals, it is very important to keep up to date with what is happening in the medium not just in terms of concepts and styles of humour but also in terms of production methods and the people and companies who are currently the movers and shakers behind the scenes. Who are the top writers and producers working in sitcom today? What has been their career history? Which companies are commissioning them, and when they submit their scripts, how are they laid out and which software do they use? As we'll discuss in more detail in our next chapter, it is also well worth keeping an eye on the up-and-coming writers and concepts – if you can recognise a new direction before it really takes off, you may be able to join the first wave of new writers who make a name for themselves fulfilling the demand for a similar product.

A case in point is the growth of the 'mockumentary' style sitcom instigated by the success of *The Office* in both its UK and US versions. While the style of presentation is different from traditional sitcom in that the shows are shot in a more documentary style, with suitably wobbly camera work, snatched moments of conversation and 'to camera' speeches by the main characters, the underlying structure of the episodes is still a lot closer to traditional sitcom plotting than it may appear. To produce this kind of material effectively the writer needs to be as familiar with the visual conventions of the type of 'reality' programming being parodied as with the conventions of sitcom writing. As already noted, the modern comedy writer is often called upon to produce material which is a 'bedrock' on top of which there is scope for the actors in a sitcom or the comedians in a topical comedy show to improvise their own material. It is often knowing that there is some workable material already there which gives the performers the 'safety net' to push the envelope and the production company the confidence to back the show. Just as with the 'oohs' and 'aahs' that Frankie Howerd used, what seems spontaneous and improvised in these new types of show is often scripted tightly beforehand and the skills of the writer, performers and directors are best demonstrated by their ability to make it look like everything is happening live and on the spot.

At the time of writing the genre of 'structured reality', as seen in shows like *Jersey Shore* and *The Only Way is Essex*, is becoming increasingly popular. Unlike mockumentary which features actors improvising from scripts, this format features non-actors as the 'stars' and is loosely based on the real events of their lives, with locations changed, dialogue 'coached' and real interactions and conversations 'reshot' in more structured ways to make them more dramatic or comedic. Whether or not you are a fan of this kind of show – and many writers bemoan the fact that reality TV in general has eaten up huge swathes of airtime once reserved for scripted comedy, and that the writers for these shows are often uncredited – it demonstrates that there will always be a need for good scriptwriters.

The other major factor in the development of scripted comedy is the growth of the internet, which has finally give writers of all kinds the ability to reach their audience without necessarily relying on a 'big break' from outside sources, as well as giving traditional show producers the opportunity to add extra ideas and nuances to their work which wouldn't fit into the standard half-hour format. A good example of the latter approach occurred when the *Scrubs* show switched channels from NBC to ABC for its final season. The new television episodes were accompanied by online-only 'webisodes' – essentially short comedy sketches featuring new and old characters from the broadcast show. In terms of writers promoting their own work, whether simply selling their services or launching professional quality short films and even sitcoms entirely online, the online world has become a hugely important career-building tool. In our next chapter we will turn our attention to your overall writing career and how best to develop it. As with your scriptwriting, the direction in which you take your career is very much up to you, but having a sound knowledge of the fundamentals will give you the maximum chance of making your own sitcom ending a happy one.

Over to you . . .

1 Select a current sketch-based comedy show or a current sitcom, preferably one which is in production right now. Produce a series of sketches or a sample episode sticking as closely as you can to the original in terms of style and also take into account practical matters – average number of scenes, average length of scenes, the strengths and personality of the featured performers, etc. Once you have finished, leave your work to one side for a couple of days until you are less 'close' to it.

2 Watch an episode of the show you have written for, then read through your own material. Then watch another episode of the existing show. What elements of your own script feel different from the actual show? It may be certain lines of dialogue, or the 'flow' of the story or humour, or maybe one of the topics you have chosen doesn't quite fit. Whatever the differences are you'll have a much better chance of spotting them when you 'surround' your work with examples of the show itself.

3 If, having made the changes, you feel your script is close enough to the original to show to the producers, or if the exercise has given you confidence that you can develop your own show idea for what is a currently popular type of show, by all means consider making an actual pitch. But read through our tips on submitting material in the next chapter to increase the possibility of getting a positive response.

6

Your Comedy Writing Career

Just as learning to write comedy is a process of trial and error, with the emphasis on error, carving out your individual comedy career is a task for which there really isn't a set blueprint. Yes, there are more sources of information on the actual writing process than there used to be, from behind-the-scenes interviews with writers, to writing classes either online or in adult education centres or colleges, to books like this one. I would certainly encourage you to use as many of these resources as possible – which is why our final chapter will include a collection of information links and suggested further reading to get you started – but when it comes to the actual business of making money from your writing, ask any group of comedy writers how they have managed it and you are liable to get as many answers as there are members of the group.

Some will be writers only, some will be writer-performers. Some will work exclusively in the writing and entertainment industry. Many will have 'day jobs' of different sorts. You will come across writers who have experienced success relatively early, and in some cases may be struggling to maintain that original momentum. Equally you may encounter writers who have been in the business for a long time, perhaps even dating back to the classic comedy eras we have referred to elsewhere in the book – but here too you are likely to find that for many, the kind of comedy they used to write and the markets they used to work in may have changed or disappeared altogether and they have often had to turn their hand to other areas of work. You will of course hear about people who got their 'break' through friends of friends or by knowing somebody in the business, and certainly any way into an industry is an advantage. But those who have lasted in the comedy industry are usually the people who had put a lot of work in before their big break so that when it came they were ready, or if they really were lucky enough to break in accidentally they had done some very fast learning since then to bring their game up to a standard where they could turn that initial opportunity into more sustainable success.

The rise of the internet has certainly enabled writers, along with other creative artists, to divide their efforts between the often long-term process of 'pushing against the right doors' in the industry in the hope that they will one day open, and being able to present their own material directly to the waiting world in the meantime. However, there are countless thousands of other people online also vying for the world's attention, so having a game plan is even more important for today's comedy writer even when they are fully 'tech savvy'. Your personal game plan is one only you can create but in my own career and also in my role as careers advisor to *The Stage* newspaper, which involves working with a wide range of creative and performing artists on developing their businesses, I have found it very useful to apply the same business planning principles to your writing career as you would if you were setting up a business in any other field.

In this chapter we will look at some of the business areas you will need to start thinking about and acting on, and in the final exercises help you apply this knowledge to your own career.

Researching the market

In Chapter Two we did a quick survey of some of the many markets open to the working comedy writer. If you have read this far into the book and, more importantly, have put some time into working through the exercises for yourself, you should by now have a good idea of which areas of comedy writing best suit your talents, which areas appeal to you most, and hopefully which areas you realistically feel you have a chance of breaking into. You may have already started your detailed research into these markets but if not now is the time to do so.

A word of caution before you begin. As we now live in the 'information age', the challenge for the new comedy writer is not so much finding out any information at all (as it used to be for those of us who started off in pre-online days), but knowing where to find *useful* information quickly and how to filter out the avalanche of useless and misleading information that is likely to come flooding your way as soon as you start your research. The creative industry is particularly prone to this danger, which is not surprising given that it is a very insecure profession. Be aware then that while connecting with other writers and performers either in person or online can be genuinely supportive, encouraging and informative, it can also open you up to a whirlwind of Chinese whispers, half-truths and pieces of sheer mythology that unfortunately pass for 'career information' in many artistic circles.

So while it is interesting to see what people are talking about on internet forums, comedy fan sites and backstage in clubs and theatres, make it your business to keep up to date on what is actually going on by consulting more authoritative sources. The trade publications for the entertainment industry are a good place to start. Many performers limit their reading of these publications, either in paper form or online, to the jobs section. A much smarter move is to keep an eye on the news and features section. It's here that you will find the answers to some of the questions we suggested you ask in previous chapters. Who is currently the person commissioning comedy at the major networks? Which companies are having shows commissioned right now? Which types of comedy show have done best ratings-wise in the last season – a good indicator that producers and networks may be looking for more of this kind of show? Equally, if a certain style of show or a former ratings winner is not being recommissioned and your current project is in a similar vein, it may be an indicator that your efforts are best directed elsewhere.

The same 'What if?' thinking you use to develop your comedy can help to develop your career. You read a news story that a certain television company which produces comedy or light entertainment type shows has been commissioned to produce a new season or a new strand of programming for the network.

The shows are due to air a year from now, but it is certainly not a good idea to wait a year before you pitch your services to the company. It's quite likely they have existing relationships with writers, but have they considered producing 'webisodes' to tie in with their programming? If not, maybe it's a suggestion you can make right now, and even if they have already had the idea, perhaps they haven't allocated a writer yet. As another example you may read that somebody who headed up production at one company is moving to take over a producing or commissioning post at another channel. Take a look back at that person's work in their previous role – did they commission and have success with particular types of show? It may be that they will be interested in introducing similar projects to this new channel. Can you use your analysis skills to come up with some ideas in that style?

Keep an eye out also for the 'rising stars' in the industry, both in front of or behind the cameras. They won't be household names as yet, and they may not get more than a mention or two on the inside pages of the trade press, but if you spot their names coming up more and more often and can see that their careers are on the up, bear in mind that, just like you, they may be looking for that breakthrough project and maybe you are the writer who can help them deliver it.

Do you spot that a particular sitcom pilot 'was commissioned based on the writer's one-act play at the X Theatre or the Y Festival'? That should be enough to get you searching for the details of next year's new plays season at that theatre or festival. By the way, one big myth you can ignore from the start is that 'professionals' will somehow be lowering themselves by entering competitions or talent contests – *every* chance you get to practise and show off your writing should be sought out and grabbed with both hands. If nothing else, competitions give you deadlines by which to get your writing projects completed and that is a great motivator to be productive.

In all the above cases you'll have spotted that the emphasis is on you doing the donkey work rather than finding somebody to make it all happen for you. Not every issue of a trade magazine or every visit to an industry website will throw up something you can use, so perseverance and patience is very much a key factor in your research. In return for your hard work, approaching things this way puts the power in your own hands to move your career forwards instead of waiting for some mysterious benefactor who may never appear.

What about comedy and TV career seminars, online courses and e-books, networking events and other 'paid for' ways of studying the business? As with any other product you are buying (this book included), be clear on what you want to get out of it before investing your money, and also make sure that the people you are paying to hear or meet are currently making a success of the career they are claiming to teach you about – not just from selling e-books, seminars and courses. They don't necessarily have to be a household name – in fact you can sometimes learn more from somebody who is just one step beyond you in terms of where you want to be in your own career than from somebody who was a huge success years ago or who is still a big name but actually developed their career in a very different market from the one that exists today. Before handing over your money, don't be at all shy to ask direct 'what have you worked on, what are you working on now, and what kind of work have you helped other people get?' type questions. If you don't get straight answers which you are able to confirm via your own research, maybe your money would be better spent elsewhere.

Often the most successful, or at least the most consistently busy writers are doing just that – writing – and are either too busy or too humble to offer advice, but that doesn't mean they won't appreciate being politely told that you have been taking a genuine interest in their career and have been seriously studying their work. With that in mind, if there is a particular writer whose work you admire, by all means let them know. If they don't have their own website or some other online contact, you can probably contact them via their agent or via the last production company they worked for.

You will, of course, be studying your role models to see what they do and what they don't do and what techniques you might learn from them for your own work, but in terms of contact with them I suggest you send no more than a short note of appreciation and perhaps mention briefly that you are aiming to break into the business yourself and what you have done so far. You may receive a polite reply or you may receive no reply at all. If you get anything more than that and any indication that the writer is willing to share some of their knowledge be very grateful and treat this valuable offer with care. There may be one particular question you would like their answer to so just send that one rather than a whole sheaf of queries. You might ask them to give an opinion on a very short example of your own work – but ask their permission before sending the work itself because, as we will see in more detail shortly, copyright is a very big issue these days. If you do get some useful answers or some feedback on your work – again, that's great, but don't push things. Thank them for what you have learned, and perhaps get back in touch in six months or a year's time to keep them updated on your progress, especially if their advice has made a difference. But whatever you do, don't bombard them with constant correspondence and requests, and certainly don't ask them for their list of work contacts. The inspiration to develop your career may come from your comedy heroes but the responsibility for developing it rests with you.

Submitting material

At the start of your writing career there are probably two broad types of submission you will be sending to clients and potential clients. The first kind is sample or 'speculative' material where you are not sure there is a job going but you want to show what you can do in case one does become available. The second kind is targeted work you have done for a particular person, show or production company. You may have invested time and effort in doing this in the hope that they will be impressed enough to use you or your script, or perhaps you have already been asked to do the work, either because the company is actually recruiting or because, having seen your previous work, they have given you your first trial job.

The quality of your writing is what will mark you out as a talent worth taking seriously, but the professionalism or otherwise with which you present that writing and any other promotional material will be the first thing they make a judgement about. In the comedy and entertainment industry first impressions are the ones which tend to stick, so it is vital to get this right.

One big change to the media world since the first edition of this book came out is that unless you are specifically asked for hard copies, the medium via which you will be submitting your writing is likely to be electronic, either via email or on disk. In terms of initial contact, I still believe there are times when a polite and well written letter on actual notepaper can be just as effective as an email, not least because people rarely receive well-written letters these days. But in terms of script material any writer with serious ambitions in today's industry needs to be familiar with the basics of email and working online. As it happens, the marks of professionalism in submitting work in paper or electronic form are not as different as they might at first seem – in both cases you are aiming to submit your work in a way that shows you value it, or else you can't expect anyone else to value it. Correct spelling, proper layout, clean packaging and as little unnecessary extra material as possible are your watchwords. Ensure your emailed work is virus checked and in a format that can be easily opened and you will be on the right track. I was in two minds whether I actually needed to say a word about submitting material in handwritten form, but I still occasionally see people doing it – so here is that word: don't.

Rule number two is to make sure you are submitting something to *somebody who can actually make use of it*. Many submissions from writers in many genres get rejected, not because of quality and not because of standard of presentation, but simply because they are sent to the wrong place. No matter how brilliant your crime novel is, you won't get it published if you send it to a publisher or agent who only handles non-fiction. Similarly, there is no point sending your sitcom pitch to a company which only produces talk shows. If you have done your research properly you shouldn't make this mistake, but companies and individuals sometimes change focus, which is why keeping up to date on the industry is so important.

Whatever market you are targeting, one of the most common concerns for beginning writers is exactly what format they should submit jokes, sketches and scripts in – that is, what they should look like when they are typed up. I'm wary of making any one-size-fits-all statements here as most individual performers, production companies and networks have their own preferred formats, types of writing software and methods of working, and they can all change as rapidly as technology does. You may be able to make a polite enquiry via email or phone to see what format the particular client or prospective client prefers, and some broadcasters already have writer's guides which provide this information. But even though there are variations in the way scripts are written from company to company and from country to country, the basic layout of a script is fairly easy to learn from books, from online examples or from templates built into writing software. As long as you observe the basic watchwords of neatness, accuracy and good spelling, if your writing is what the client is excited about, they won't reject you just because the format needs a little tweaking.

Keep a note of when you sent your work and who you sent it to. You may want to call or email after a week or so to make sure your work has arrived, but bearing in mind that people in the media receive a huge amount of unsolicited material every week, don't be at all surprised if it takes a long time to get a response or feedback. With some of the bigger companies six months is not an unusual wait time, so rather than waiting for an answer, keep busy with your own marketing and working on your next projects.

We'll talk a little about your personal branding when it comes to your web presence but in terms of submitting you and your work to clients, 'businesslike' is the way to go. You don't have to make your business card or letterhead look like a chartered accountant's (and you certainly should invest in a decent business card and create a nice letterhead for yourself) but avoid overtly jokey designs and typefaces – you want to deliver the message

'I'm a professional', not 'I'm a wacky person who is trying really, really hard to be funny'. The same applies to your email address. It makes sense to create an email for your work which separates it from your personal one. By all means create one which indicates that you are a writer if you would like to (although simply using your name is fine too), but avoid anything too loud or 'crazy', not least because as well as creating the wrong impression it may lead to your hard work ending up in a spam filter.

Speaking of losing work, note that although computer technology continues to develop in leaps and bounds, that often just means there are even more ways for your writing to disappear if you don't save it properly. Computer crashes, virus problems, corrupt files – if disaster is going to strike it will always obey the sitcom rule of striking at the worst possible time. Just after I had completed half of the previous chapter of this book with the final submission deadline looming, my computer suddenly and unceremoniously died. If I had not emailed a copy to myself literally thirty seconds before the screen went blank, there might well have been a large 6,000-word gap in the pages you are holding in your hand.

Imitation – the sincerest form of larceny

One concern that writers both old and new have when submitting work is important enough to merit its own section: 'What if somebody steals my ideas?' I can remove any doubts or uncertainty you may have on this topic very easily. If you are producing good comedy for any length of time people are *guaranteed* to steal your ideas. On the live comedy circuit gag-stealing has always been rife. In the online world, good jokes travel across the world in seconds, and wars constantly break out across Twitter and other social websites as to who stole which line from who. As we have already discussed when talking about joke writing, adaptation and working with existing structures have always been part and parcel of comedy writing. In the area of topical humour it is very possible for two entirely different people to think up the same line at more or less the same time. So unless you want to do as an American comedian on tour in the UK some years ago allegedly did, and set about a supposed 'gag thief' with a large plank of wood, there is not an awful lot you can do to stop people repeating and reusing your best lines. Best to view it as an indication that you are good at what you do and get busy with writing even better lines.

That said, even I would have to agree that having entire programme ideas swiped is a lot more serious and frustrating than just losing the occasional one-liner. The traditional method of proving that you have written a particular piece on a specific date has always been to mail a hard copy to yourself, keep it unopened when it arrives and keep your record of the posting date. Latterly there are various physical and online registration services which offer, for varying fees, to confirm your ownership should the need ever arise. An even better way I have found is simply to keep your mouth shut about projects you are working on unless you are talking to or showing them to somebody you know you can trust. Even then keeping quiet can be a good plan – most writers are closet performers whether they ever actually get on stage or not, and often the energy in our work comes from the fact that we are so excited about telling our stories. Sometimes telling them too often before we have actually written them can dissipate that energy.

Costly legal disputes can and do arise over the originality of successful media properties, which is why production companies are becoming more and more wary of copyright issues. This can make it a lot harder to send unsolicited work as a writer. Many companies simply won't accept it unless it is submitted via an agent, while other companies and some agents won't look at work unless the writer first signs a lengthy disclaimer renouncing any right to sue should there be any question of possible copyright infringement in the future. Whether or not you agree to these conditions depends very much on how keen you are to work with the people insisting on them.

Another possible scenario is that a writer submits a script or idea to a company, and while they like the basic concept, they want to develop it using one of their own people. I am talking here about reputable companies who will make a decent offer for the rights to develop the property further without the original writer being involved. It is unlikely most writers will be pleased with this outcome but it is worth getting sensible legal advice from somebody who knows the industry well before accepting or rejecting the offer. It would obviously be a shame to sell the idea for what might seem like a lot of money but turns out to be very little if the project becomes a hit. Equally it would be a shame to let ego get in the way of making some money from an idea which may actually never get developed (this is the outcome for most projects which get 'optioned') but as a result perhaps developing a contact within a company which can be built on so that your next project is taken on with you on board.

If you want my own non-legal opinion, the best plan on the copyright issue is to get good advice from people who know what they are talking about when you do have specific concerns about deals you are offered, but ultimately to get on with your writing and work on developing a style and reputation that is so obviously yours that nobody can steal it, rather than wasting your energy assuming that everybody in the industry is out to get you and ready to rip you off.

Not quite the world's oldest profession . . .

When you originally start your comedy writing career you may have no contacts, no place to work and nobody crying out for your material. While the most important factor in changing this situation is going to be your own motivation and self-belief, I will be delighted if some of the ideas in this book make a difference too.

Do bear in mind though that success can also bring its own pressures and responsibilities. For me, the major difference I have experienced in the journey from being a beginner to a professional writer is the contrast between the times in the past when I had to motivate myself to turn out jokes, scripts and sketch ideas when nobody seemed particularly interested, and the unavoidable occasions now when too many deadlines collide at once, I may have several pieces of work to get finished in a very short time and I wish I had been a little more careful about what I wished for in the first place.

In order to minimise these occasions, and to cope when they do happen, I have found that while, like many creative people, I am not a naturally organised person, the more organised I can be, the easier it is to maintain my professionalism. And the more professional a writer is, the more chance there is that work will continue to come in as each existing project is completed. As with any freelance profession – and the majority of writers are freelance – you are only as good as your last job, and the most dangerous thing you can do when things are going well is to become sloppy and start to rest on your laurels.

You might be doing very well in your career – the shows you are working on are topping the ratings and everybody wants you to come and work for them. Then one of your shows drops in the ratings, the lead actor in another project moves to Hollywood, or a new commissioning editor turns up and brings in the team they worked with at their previous channel. Like most writers I have had enough ups and downs in my career to know that it is very important to find the balance between two equally important aspects of your comedy career: doing the best job you can with the work you are currently doing and also doing all you can to find new projects and opportunities for the future so that all your career eggs are not in the one basket.

You may never appear on stage yourself but nevertheless as a comedy writer you are part of showbusiness, and the golden rule of this business is that no matter what happens the show must go on. The show definitely can't go on without your words being delivered on time, and you won't find many people anxious to work with you on a regular basis if you develop a reputation for missing deadlines. Even when you are diligent in the way you work, there are always times when something unexpected happens and you have to pull out all the stops and go the extra mile.

I have had to rewrite a children's show episode just an hour before filming when the cast changed at the last minute, and on one occasion before the advent of the internet, run around Edinburgh in the early morning trying to find a fax machine, because the show I was writing topical gags for back in London hadn't received the fax I had sent the night before. As a professional, that wasn't their problem – it was mine. Although I didn't manage to find a fax machine until the show had been on the air for half an hour, I have no doubt that it was the fact that I accepted responsibility for the problem and did everything I could to solve it which meant I was kept on as the show's writer.

Just as you should know your strengths as a writer, you should be aware of your limitations too. At the beginning of your career it makes sense to try everything, but as your journey progresses you'll have a better idea of what you do well and what others can do better and, very importantly, how long it will realistically take you to do certain kinds of work.

It can be very tempting to accept every job offered just to get your work used, but if I was offered a job which I really didn't feel I could do well, I think I would rather politely decline and if possible recommend somebody more suited (industry knowledge pays off here too) rather than say yes and deliver substandard work or miss the deadline.

On that point do remember to overestimate deadlines if you can – allow time for rewrites and for things to go wrong ahead of time and you will have fewer 'heart attack' moments and, more importantly, give fewer heart attack moments to people you are hoping will want to hire you again in the future.

Finances

If comedy is about truth, it is important to be truthful about the financial aspect of comedy too. So let me be truthful and say that while I have enjoyed my time as a comedy writer, I wouldn't necessarily recommend it as one of the most secure ways of earning an income even by the generally insecure standards of working in the entertainment industry.

In comedy, as in many other fields of creativity, there are far fewer restrictions on content than there used to be with regard to sexuality, political incorrectness or any other taboo, but whenever I give talks to young writers or performers I'm aware that there is one question which may be running through their heads but which they are still very reluctant to express out loud – how much do you earn from comedy writing?

The answer is that like many freelance artists and writers I have had periods in my career when I have worked for little more than expenses and other times when I've been paid very handsomely indeed for stuff which wasn't all that different from the work I used to do for nothing. I've had staff jobs on programmes and publications when I was paid a set amount regularly, and other contracts where I was paid a larger amount of money all in one go. Television work in particular is known for large fees, although this isn't necessarily the case for non-primetime shows. Even the projects which do pay a lot are often relatively short-term contracts. £20,000 for a few weeks' work may sound like a lot of money, but for many writers and performers, those few weeks of work can quite easily be their only significant employment for the year, out of which they still have to pay taxes and agent commission. That's why for most writers the 'day job' is an important element in allowing them to take time out to write, and finding the right one can be just as important a step in building your career as the more creative side to your work.

Some beginners tell me that they are worried that if they have a full-time or part-time job they won't have any energy left for writing at the end of the day. For the reasons mentioned above I always respond by reminding them that it is very hard to be funny when you are up to your ears in debt and trying to write on an empty stomach. I also think a day job contributes to, rather than detracts from, your writing in the sense that given that the best comedy connects with ordinary people, the more contact you have with the real world instead of staring at a computer screen or swanning around TV studios all day, the better.

So assuming you have managed to find paid writing work, what do you charge for it? We'll discuss how an agent might help very shortly, but if you are the one doing the negotiating the fact that there is no real going rate for comedy writing and that even if there was most comedy writers would die rather than share the information can make things a bit difficult. The best thing you can do is research the rates for similar types of work as best you can. State bodies like the BBC and industry associations like the National Union of Journalists have set rates for writing work (although big names obviously get paid above this rate) and investigating these may give you a ballpark figure to start off with. Another useful way to make your decision is to decide how many hours the work will take you, and then decided how much you are prepared to work for per hour and negotiate on that basis. While you are finding out about writers' rates do some research on royalties, overseas sales and rerun rights also, so that you don't miss out on these income sources.

Companies which regularly commission writers may well have set rates and that is what you will be offered. These rates may still be negotiable, but whatever you finally agree to, make sure you get a contract in writing and, once you have got it, make sure you read it carefully before signing. If there is a lot of money or work involved it may well be worth the investment to get somebody who knows the law, and preferably the law relating to writers and broadcast, to look over the contract for you. Whether you yourself or a legal expert do this, don't just focus on the upfront payments – keep an eye out for clauses relating to ownership of characters and ideas, rewrite arrangements, merchandising and online rights and all the other little clauses which might seem unimportant in your excitement to get going on the project but can return to bite you later.

Speaking of getting bitten, if you are starting to make money from your comedy writing, you will need to have a chat with your local tax official before they decide to have a chat with you. You don't want to get paid a large lump sum one year, have a long break before your next job, and then discover that when the tax man comes looking for his share of the big payment you have had to spend it on basic necessities. On a brighter note, if you need to buy materials to use in your writing career, including computer supplies and even comedy DVDs for research, you may be able to claim the expenses back at tax-return time.

There's no people like show people . . .

As well as being the 'hardest job in the world', writing or performing comedy has also been described as one of the loneliest jobs in the world. But in actual fact your comedy writing success will be just as much down to your ability to deal with people as your facility with words. Earlier in the book we touched on your relationship with the performers you might work with, but here are some other people you may come across, with some thoughts on the best way of working with each one.

Writing partners

You may or may not want to work with a writing partner. While many of the most successful British comedy writers have worked in teams, from Galton and Simpson to Ronald Wolfe and Ronald Chesney, and with team-writing in the US now the norm rather than the exception, there are also successful writers like John Sullivan or Roy Clarke who have produced long-running hit series working alone. Theatrical satirist Howard Brenton maintains that comedy works best when there are two authors: 'You have to speak the gags aloud to see if your partner's eyes go dead.' A less artistic but just as understandable motivation is that writing of any sort tends to be a very solitary activity and you may just want somebody else to work with to make it more sociable. Whatever your decision on whether or not you work with a partner (and it can be a good experience to try even if you eventually decide to work alone), a similar conversation, and a follow-up letter of agreement, as we recommended when we discussed forming a writing relationship with a comedy performer, will make life a lot easier for both of you.

When searching for a suitable partner, or when a prospective partnership presents itself, it is also worth considering that the strongest comedy partnerships are like marriages – the sum of talents involved should be greater than either could produce working alone. With that in mind, I have realised that some of the partnerships I have had in the past with people who are very like me have been great fun, but in all honesty the end results were something either of us could have produced by ourselves, whereas some of the most productive and successful writing projects I have been involved in are with people for whom I have a tremendous amount of respect, and who I very much enjoyed working with, but who were often very different from me in sense of humour and approach to the work. Inevitably compromises had to be made on both sides, but the end results and the learning experience, for me at least, were well worth the effort in that both of us were stretched to produce work outside our comfort zones.

Agents

Just as we sometimes think it might be nice to have a writing partner for the simple comfort of knowing we haven't got to forge our path alone, it sounds very attractive to have an agent who is out there working for us, promoting our talent, and getting us lots of lucrative contracts for top TV money and maybe even a few movie deals thrown in. It's quite possible that a top agent will be able to do all of those things, but the problem at the beginning of our careers is that getting a top agent is a bit of a 'Catch 22' aspiration. The agents who can actually open doors already have established writers on their books, and are usually reluctant to take on new clients, particularly unpublished ones. After all, if you were an agent and only made your living by getting a relatively small percentage of somebody else's earnings, who would you be more likely to spend the bulk of your time promoting: a first-time comedy writer or an established name who is in talks for a thirteen-part drama series?

As the chances of landing a top agent straight off are somewhat slim, that leaves three other options. Option number one is to promote yourself, and this is one I heartily recommend everyone try at some point even if getting an agent is your eventual goal. Not only does it makes sense to know at first hand exactly how much work is involved in promoting yourself so that you can make sure your agent does it properly when you do hire one (and remember an agent works for you, not the other way round), but the chances of an agent being interested in you are greatly increased once you can demonstrate that you are already capable of earning money from your work. Option number two is to accept any agent who wants to take you, but this is usually an option to be avoided because, as we have already noted, the agents you want to work with don't usually come looking for clients. They certainly never charge upfront fees for being your agent, and any offers you get which suggest this, no matter how flattering they are about your talent and how many big promises they make, should be rejected out of hand. This leaves one last option, which is to find an agent who may not be one of the high-flyers, but has a small number of writers or performers on their books and on their website who may not be making a fortune but who are working steadily. A smaller agent may be more willing to invest time in building their clients' careers and, if you have already done the agent chores for yourself, you should have a much better idea of how to spot that kind of agent once you are in discussion with them.

As with any other business relationship, you and your agent should have a clear agreement in writing about who does what and for how much. The right agent is not just valuable in finding you work, they can also be very useful sounding boards in terms of what work would be best for you in the long term, be busy protecting your interests when you are in the middle of doing a job, and do their best to bring each job you do get to the attention of the right people in the industry to make sure it leads to more work.

Actors, producers, directors, editors

Co-writers and agents are people you may or may not choose to work with throughout your career. But given that we writers spend a lot of time by ourselves in the actual writing process, it can sometimes be easy to forget that we are only one part of the wider creative process and that inevitably involves other people. The more we can learn about the other people who are involved in this process, the better. Whenever you do get a chance to visit

189

a set or a studio, either because of your own work or simply as an observer or audience member, keep your eyes and ears open. Learn as much as you can not just about your job but about everyone else's. Be interested in other people, even the more anonymous ones such as scene shifters and camera operators, and you will be surprised how many tips you can pick up that will help your writing. Even if your career does take off, stay humble and grounded – the person who brings you your coffee on set today may be the producer or commissioning editor you are pitching your work to in five years' time. If you ever get a chance to sit with an editor while they are working on a comedy show, grab it with both hands – in today's broadcast world the way a show is edited can make or break it almost more than any other single element beyond the script and acting themselves. The best writers are not only always creating, they are always learning – and everyone you work with has something to teach you.

Which brings us to one final group of people who have more influence on your success or failure than anyone else . . .

The audience

In previous decades and indeed in previous editions of this book, there were very few ways to bring your work to a mass audience that didn't involve waiting for either permission or funding or both from a third party, usually a production company, a publisher or a TV network. The internet has changed all that, and for most comedy performers and writers has become a vital tool not only in marketing themselves within the industry but also in delivering their products directly to the audience. We have already mentioned that the internet is a mass of comedy-related marketing information via industry-related websites and blogs as well as a way of interacting directly with your audiences via social media networks and with personal websites which are not only good looking but can often be very cheap to design and maintain. Unlike websites in earlier times you can constantly change and update your website and present your biographical details, samples of your work in print, audio or video form and your contact details all in one place. You can link to other websites and increase your online traffic, and as a freelance writer you can register with a number of different websites which will alert you when suitable jobs become available, as well as allowing potential clients to contact you when they have work that might suit your talents.

As with any other business tool, the web has its challenges as well as its advantages. To keep your web marketing fresh it needs to be regularly updated – which is more time that you'll need to juggle with your actual writing. Try to be realistic: it is better to update your blog or tweet regularly once or twice a week rather than promise to do it daily and then taper off to nothing in a week or two. It is easy to start with enthusiasm and then lose heart. There are millions of other web users competing for attention and it can take time to build up even a small regular following.

For anyone who has been put off doing stand-up for fear of being heckled, you need to be aware that having any sort of public presence on the web is an open invitation to the cowardliest hecklers of all – the anonymous 'flamers' who will almost certainly leave negative 'reviews', post sarcastic comments and rush to press the 'dislike' button whenever they get the chance. Sadly, but not surprisingly, the comedy world is particularly prone to jealous and resentful types whose only comedy 'talent' appears to be in knocking the work of others. Whether you choose to read or ignore this sort of comment on public sites, and whether your policy is to delete it when it shows up on your own web pages or guest books or block the senders entirely (you should certainly be too busy building your career to waste time responding), don't let them put you off making your mark online. Most of the time you will also enjoy being encouraged by the positive feedback you receive, and realising your work is reaching an audience you may never meet in person. You may even get feedback which, although critical, is offered sincerely and can point the way to better targeting your work to your audience if you are big enough to 'take it seriously but not personally'. It is usually pretty easy to work out which comments are which and in terms of the haters; nineteenth-century humorist Oscar Wilde said it best: 'The only thing worse than being talked about is not being talked about.'

You are a comedy writer . . .

When we first began brainstorming and churning out joke ideas, I mentioned that once you saw how much work was involved in developing a comedy writing career, you might not want to do it any more. I hope the fact that you have read this far means you still do and, more than that, I hope something I have suggested in these pages has made this a little more possible for you. As I told you when we started out, the material I have gathered here is by no means the only route or even the best route to achieving your aims, but it does comprise the things which I have tried and tested in my own career and which also seem to have worked for the people I coach, advise and mentor. As you continue your own journey you will no doubt come across other ideas and approaches and possibly even come up with some new ones of your own. I can only encourage you to try out every new idea at least once, so that you can find out what does and doesn't work for you.

During the course of my writing career I've had lots of wonderful days when I wouldn't have swapped working in comedy for anything else in the world. I've also had days when I wondered if anyone else was insane enough to choose this as a profession. As your career progresses you too will almost certainly have both kinds of day. But it won't be the good or bad days that make you a comedy writer. It won't even be the killer routines, hit sitcom and sketch shows or the awards and huge paydays that I sincerely wish for you.

It's the fact that unlike the 99 per cent of people who 'want to write, mean to write, would love to have written', I just know that when you finish this book you will get down to the actual business of writing. Whatever you do write, whether published or unpublished, commissioned or uncommissioned, performed in public, on the airwaves or online, you are now a comedy writer and there is no other comedy writer in the world quite like you.

So go on, then – make us laugh.

Over to you . . .

Throughout this book I have been asking you to study the work of successful writers and comedians to discover ideas and techniques you can apply to your own writing.

For this final exercise, your mission is to study successful comedy writers from a business point of view to discover the tips which will work best for you in this area. Based on your industry research, look at current writers who are in some way similar to you in terms of style or main area of work. If possible choose people who are currently making the breakthroughs you would like to be making in a year or so rather than people who are already established or have a long career history. Find out as much as you can about these writers – their recent career history, how they market themselves online or offline, how they present themselves in any promotional material. What can you learn and apply to your own work?

If possible choose several writers to study and note what you like and don't like about each person's marketing approach. Then make your own marketing plan by working backwards – where would you like to be career-wise in two years' time? Where would you need to be in one year to have a chance of making that happen? In six months? Work back until you get to what you need to be doing now, whether it is completing your sample scripts, establishing your own web presence, starting to enter competitions, joining a comedy class or doing an open mike spot – whatever small steps you need to take to get your comedy career on the road, start taking them now.

The final chapter of this book includes some useful resources to get you started.

Appendix

The Comedy Writer's Resource Kit

When it comes to learning to write comedy, the most important 'resources' are the same as they have always been: your determination to do it in the first place, and the path that has been carved out for you by the many great writers and comics who have done it before.

A decade or two ago, I might have suggested that they were almost the *only* resources available to the budding comedy writer, but that is certainly a situation that has changed more recently. There are now quite a few courses, full-time and part-time, academic and non-academic, devoted to comedy writing and performing. There are also a wide variety of books, a whole archive of video and audio recordings and an ever-growing internet treasure trove of international resources, most of which can be accessed at the click of a mouse.

However, just as a piece of comedy writing, no matter how many university degrees it is accompanied by, isn't funny unless it makes an audience laugh, a 'resource' isn't actually useful unless it works for you. All I can do in the space available here is list some of the discoveries I have personally made, and some of the books and links which have been most useful to me. As internet sites can disappear overnight, I've focused on the ones which can act as portals to many other useful sites and resources. I'm pretty sure that, whatever problems you may face or further questions you may have as you develop your own career, the solution is already out there somewhere. It's part of your challenge as a writer to use your creative thinking and determination to find it. Here are some suggestions to help you begin your search:

Books

Perret, Gene, *The New Comedy Writing Step by Step*. Fresno: Quill Driver Books, 2007
This book deserves a very special mention as Gene is the 'Godfather' of structured comedy writing. As well as being Bob Hope's head writer, he has written for Bill Cosby, Phyllis Diller and many others. He has also been involved in writing many top-rated US sitcoms. Gene's books on comedy writing were among the first to attempt to break down the 'mystique' of the art form and make it accessible to beginners, and they are still among the most practical and comprehensive in the world. Precisely because they are so detailed, and often involve exercises and challenges for the reader to complete, they can sometimes seem daunting to less committed writers, but Perret's systematic approach to humour writing works, whatever your own background and level of experience and whether you see yourself as a traditionalist or modernist in the comedy field.

Other books which may be of interest include:

Murray, Logan, *Be A Great Stand-Up*. London: Teach Yourself, 2010
Holloway, Sally, *The Serious Guide to Joke Writing*. Great Yarmouth: Bookshaker, 2010
Kind, Andy, *Stand Up and Deliver*. Oxford: Monarch Books, 2011
Ashton, Paul, *The Calling Card Script*. London: A&C Black, 2011
Helitzer, Melvin, *Comedy Writing Secrets*. Cincinnati: Writer's Digest Books, 1992

Practising any style of writing, whether parodied or played straight, can only help your comedy writing. To this end you may wish to check out the rest of the *Writing Handbook* series published by Bloomsbury (formerly published by A&C Black) and uniform with this one.

Writers' and Artists' Yearbook, published annually by A&C Black, has a comprehensive list of TV and radio companies, writers' agents and which areas they cover, and much useful information on the general business of making it as a writer.

Contacts (published by *The Spotlight*) is the place to find a list of theatrical/TV agents.
For US agents try www.agentassociations.com

Writing resources and organisations

The British Society of Comedy Writers
www.bscw.co.uk

The Writers' Guild of Great Britain
www.writersguild.org.uk

The Society of Authors
www.societyofauthors.org

BBC writersroom
www.bbc.co.uk/writersroom

Industry information

The Stage (national newspaper of the UK entertainment industry)
www.thestage.co.uk

The Spotlight (good resource for tracking down performers' agents)
www.the-spotlight.co.uk

Variety (national newspaper of the US entertainment industry)
www.variety.com

Broadcast magazine
www.broadcastnow.co.uk

Media UK directory
www.mediauk.com

Scriptwriting software and resources

www.thescreenwritersstore.net
(website for The Screenwriter's Store with a wide selection of books and packages)

Comedy websites

www.chortle.co.uk

www.funnyordie.com

www.rooftopcomedy.com

www.archive.org
(This site features a vast amount of classic US radio and TV recordings dating as far back as the 1920s.)

Many of the major broadcasting networks on both sides of the Atlantic are now making their back catalogue of programmes available online. Visit the broadcasters' individual websites to check what is available, and what can be accessed from your home territory.

Self-publishing resources

www.lulu.com

www.cafepress.com

www.blogspot.com

Comedy to study

Comedy is a very subjective thing, and popular surveys tend to be biased towards contemporary names, but to help you with your comedy research, here are the results of a number of 'best comedy' surveys, starting with the top twenty names (in reverse order, of course) from Channel 4 TV's survey of the top 100 'greatest' stand-up comedians.

20	Jasper Carrott
19	Les Dawson
18	Alexei Sayle
17	Dylan Moran
16	Al Murray
15	Jerry Sadowitz
14	Woody Allen
13	Jack Dee
12	Jimmy Carr
11	Ricky Gervais
10	Ross Noble
9	Chris Rock
8	Victoria Wood
7	Bill Bailey
6	Bill Hicks
5	Harry Hill
4	Richard Pryor
3	Eddie Izzard
2	Peter Kay
1	Billy Connolly

Here are the names which made the top twenty from a similar but US-based survey (for the Comedy Central Channel) but which are not repeated in the UK list: George Carlin, Lenny Bruce, Chris Rock, Steve Martin, Rodney Dangerfield, Bill Cosby, Roseanne Barr, Eddie Murphy, Johnny Carson, Jerry Seinfeld, Robin Williams, Bob Newhart, David Letterman, Ellen DeGeneres, Don Rickles, Jonathan Winters, Sam Kinison.

The top ten shows from the BBC's survey of most popular British sitcoms:

Only Fools and Horses
Blackadder
The Vicar of Dibley
Dad's Army
Fawlty Towers
Yes Minister
Porridge
Open All Hours
The Good Life
One Foot In The Grave

There are a huge number of similar lists for American sitcoms so you will have to visit a few and make your own choices. www.imdb.com is one place to start looking, and if you don't agree with any of the lists, feel free to compile and upload your own.

Comedy courses and writing classes

Search classes in your local area at www.hotcourses.com (UK) and www.hotcoursesusa.com (USA)

Keep in touch . . .

Thanks for taking this comedy journey with me. And now it really is over to you. Every success and please do keep me posted on your progress at johnbyrnecontact@gmail.com

Index